friendship Reset

"By now most of us have heard that young people—despite being constantly connected online—are lonelier than ever and consistently report having few real friends. In *Friendship Reset*, Maggie Craig addresses this crisis head-on and offers a timeless and true remedy to isolation and loneliness: friendship. With wisdom, humor, and memorable personal stories, Craig shows her readers what a friend is, what a friend is not, how to be a good friend, how to make friends, and even how to end a friendship. This little book will serve as a helpful resource for anyone working with young people in the Church today."

Fr. Damian Ference

Vicar for evangelization and secretary for parish life in the Diocese of Cleveland and professor of philosophy at Borromeo Seminary

"Friendship is a path to joy, to the rebuilding of the Church and world, and ultimately to an encounter with God. We don't take it seriously enough. And perhaps more tragically, we've forgotten how—as our parents told us when we were five—to 'make friends.' Maggie Craig reminds us why friendship matters and most importantly how to build life-changing friendships in practical ways. And all with a writing style that's strikingly accessible and enjoyable. Read this book. Then give it to a friend!"

Chris Stefanick

Evangelist, TV host, and author of *Real Life Catholic*

"A faithful friend is a strong defense, and finding one is like finding a treasure. . . . A faithful friend is also like medicine for life, and those who fear the Lord will find one" (Ecclesiastes 6:14–16). Scripture is clear: healthy, holy friendships are so important for us.

A good friend is a treasure indeed. Yet many today struggle to find the life-giving, Christ-centered friendships that we all need—that we all desire. In *Friendship Reset*, Maggie Craig gives thoughtful and practical advice on how to evaluate, cultivate, and navigate modern friendships. If you find yourself feeling confused, uncertain, or dissatisfied with your friendships, this book will be a great aid and companion to you!"

Matthew Breuninger
Associate professor of clinical psychology at
Franciscan University of Steubenville

"There's the classic joke: Jesus performed many miracles during his public ministry, but perhaps his greatest miracle was having twelve close friends. Friendship is simply hard, especially in today's digital world! However, Maggie Craig makes it much more practical and much less daunting with *Friendship Reset*."

Tanner Kalina
Catholic evangelist and author of *Aching for Greatness*

friendship Reset

Ditch the Drama and Find Your Crew

A Practical Guide for Christians

MAGGIE CRAIG

Foreword by Emily Wilson Hussem

Ave Maria Press AVE Notre Dame, Indiana

Founded in 1865, Ave Maria Press is a ministry of the United States Province of Holy Cross.

www.avemariapress.com

Paperback: ISBN-13 978-1-64680-385-9

E-book: ISBN-13 978-1-64680-386-6

Cover image © shironosov / iStock / Getty Images Plus.

Cover and text design by Samantha Watson.

Printed and bound in the United States of America.

Library of Congress Cataloging-in-Publication Data is available.

To my dearest friends, near and far. Thank you for patiently teaching me about the life-changing power of friendship.

Special love to my big sister, Louise, who is my first and forever friend.

You all have formed me into a better human, a better friend, and a better Christian. God knows what I need and I need all of you.

Contents

Foreword

For most of my life, I secretly felt like I was the only person who struggled with friendship—making friends, keeping friends, being a present friend, knowing how to be there for a friend in need. I looked around often feeling like everyone else had it figured out. Everyone had a best friend or a tight-knit group of friends that stuck together for years into adulthood, and everyone seemed to have a secret formula to cultivating and maintaining great friendships. It was not until adulthood that I realized that figuring out each of these aspects of friendship is a struggle for many people in our world today. I was not alone in this.

If you struggle with any aspect of friendship, this is the first thing I want you to know: you are not alone.

You are also not alone in your innate desire for friends! It is an inherent part of who we are to long to be seen, known, and loved unconditionally in true, meaningful relationships with others. We are crafted in the image and likeness of our almighty, unstoppable God, who is the Trinity—Father, Son, and Holy Spirit. We were made to be in relationship—this is a good and beautiful thing.

For over a dozen years, I was a diligent student who learned about math, science, writing, and many other subjects in school. But we are often left to figure out friendship on our own. There was no class called "Friendship 101" that I could select as part of my schedule in high school. We do not receive any formal education in the life skill of friendship, nor do we get a how-to on what to do when we get in a disagreement with a friend or come to a fork in the road where we feel deep down in our gut that a friendship needs to come to an end. Many of us aren't formed in how to live out mutual accountability in faith or how to talk to a friend with love about bad choices they are making. I need formation in this area. You need formation in this area. We all do!

That is why the book you hold in your hands is so important.

In the book you are about to read, Maggie is going to lovingly and authentically share with you about her own journey on the road of friendship. She will bring you into important stories and lessons she has learned over time about what it means to be a true and steady friend. You are going to receive the formation we all should have been given when we were young (in the midst of everything we learned academically) about how to practically navigate friendships. This book is chock-full of incredible examples each one of us needs in order to answer many of those questions we have . . . how do I end a friendship? What are green and red flags in a friendship? How do I communicate well as a friend in a culture of so much small talk and fear of vulnerability?

I encourage you as you begin to allow Maggie be your guide in this. Opening your heart to the words that follow will help you deepen current friendships and make new ones. Incline your ear to her stories that will stay with you and come up in moments when you may need them for encouragement and fortitude on the journey!

May God bless you with beautiful, life-giving friendships to help you know just how seen, known, and cared for you are.

May God give us the friends we need, and may we be the friend others need on their journey, too.

Emily Wilson Hussem

Introduction

I remember the first time I met up with friends after the COVID pandemic was dying down. I had spent months holed up in my apartment, capitalizing on my solo time by dutifully watering my plants, cooking experimental dishes, and brushing up on my grasp of the Spanish language. Finally when restaurants were opening back up, my friends and I enthusiastically picked a time to get together. Of course, we had stayed in touch through phone calls, video chat, and text messaging over the pandemic, but it did not compare to all of us being together in person. I couldn't wait. I wanted to laugh long and hard while consuming bottomless chips and salsa. I wanted conversation to flow easily over a wide range of topics. I wanted to soak in the warm glow of friendship that I had missed for months.

But that's not quite what happened. My friends and I ate tacos and drank margaritas. We exchanged updates. We swapped amusing stories. But everything felt stilted—overly formal. Not even thirty minutes into our meal, I wanted to put my head down and fall asleep on my refried beans. I was exhausted by the very thing I so eagerly anticipated. Driving home that night, I realized that friendship was a muscle. By the grace of God, I had developed many strong and different friendship muscles throughout the years. But through the isolation of the COVID pandemic, those muscles had atrophied. I was out of practice being a good friend. Something that used to feel so natural, like talking and listening and spending time with my friends in person, was now a challenge. But I was eager to get back in shape. I was ready to flex those friendship muscles again.

I hope you are too. Maybe your friendship muscles are feeling a little weak. Or maybe they haven't even had the chance to fully develop. Maybe you're looking for some guidance on how to navigate your social connections in a postpandemic, overdigitized world. Maybe you're struggling to unlearn the lie that it's better and safer to just be alone. Maybe the only relationships you have prioritized are romantic ones, and you want to have better friends. Maybe you're going through a transition and need to build brand-new relationships from scratch. Maybe you're noticing some unhealthy behavior in your friendships and know they need to be purified. Maybe you're looking to take your current friendships a little deeper and to have more meaningful platonic bonds.

This book is for you! It will act as your friendship field guide, and I will act as your cheerleader, dancing with my pom-poms and rallying behind you as you bravely examine your relationships. You will be given practical tips on how to make your friendships more Christ centered and ultimately fulfilling. Why should your friendships be Christ centered? Because as Christians, everything in our lives should be centered on Jesus Christ! Jesus is the way, the truth, and the life (see John 14:6). He is our guiding light in all things, most certainly including friendship. In these pages, you will find encouragement and support from a Christian perspective, as well as plenty of personal stories on how I have learned these lessons the hard way.

Why should you listen to me?

Being fully honest here: I have not always been a great friend. Nor have I spent my entire life in spectacular friendships. But my own mistakes have acted as excellent teachers, as have my own life experiences. Growing up, my family moved multiple times, and I changed schools every couple of years. Now, I am a full-time Christian speaker and I travel the world for months at a time. I say this humbly but truthfully: I am now quite accomplished at finding friends, making friends, keeping friends, and growing those friendships from the briefest of interactions to the strongest of bonds. I am convinced of the nearly unstoppable power of friendship, and I have seen its effects first-hand in my life in the most beautiful of ways. I believe in friendship, and I want you to recognize and unleash its power in your own life as well. That is what this book is about—forming and purifying friendships of the same sex. Meaning, friendships shared between women and friendships shared between men.

Can men and women be friendly with each other? Of course they can be, and they must! Men and women have much to learn from each other. They add so much humor and perspective and happiness to each other's lives. But when one man and one woman are emotionally intimate with each other and share an exclusive connection, I consider that dating. As a teenager, I struggled with this. I had several good guy friends, and I considered our closeness to be totally fine. But still, I often wondered if it was normal. Eventually I confided in a priest about my situation, saying: "I can be best friends with guys! After all, St. Francis and St. Clare were close friends!"

The priest shrewdly observed: "But neither of you care about holiness as much as St. Francis or St. Clare."

Ouch. I hated hearing what he had to say. But after I let it sink in, I knew he was right. At best, commitment-free dating masquerading as simple friendship is lazy and misleading. At worst, it's cowardly and cruel. Either it's time to take the next step and enter into a romantic relationship, or it's time to pull back and focus on forming friendships of the same sex.

Because Christians looks to Jesus as a model, they will see that Jesus spent time with women. He listened to their stories and helped them write new ones, and he certainly treasured his relationship with his mother. But there is no denying the special bond he shared between Peter, James, and John (see Mark 5:37; Luke 8:51; Matthew 26:36–38).

Men need strong friendships with each other, and so do women. This is how we are designed. Women understand women. Men understand men. And so, men are intentionally built for friendships with other men, while women are uniquely crafted for friendships with other women. They get each other on a biological level. Just as women often share similar struggles with other women, men often experience the same vices as other men. Or, at least they can relate to their motivations and circumstances. Because of this, same-sex friendships are uniquely privileged to provide the support and accountability we all need to thrive socially and spiritually.

Not everyone agrees. I have met plenty of women who shy away from friendships with other women. They claim that women are "too dramatic," and they prefer the uncomplicated companionship of men. I know men who struggle to fit into hyper-macho culture and would rather exclusively find companionship through the kindness of women. Both approaches are understandable, but potentially detrimental. This mindset may be masking a deeper hurt or a past betrayal that needs to be addressed. It also views men and women through the lens of superficial stereotypes rather than through the truth of divine design. I say this from personal experience: women may not define themselves as traditionally "girly" yet are still abundantly capable of forming friendships with other women. Men may be unable to pigeonhole themselves into the classic understanding of "manly" yet still possess the ability to share strong friendships with other men.

We need more than just familial or romantic ties. Women need female friendships. Men need male friendships. Human beings need friendships. Healthy romantic relationships have their time and their place (which is probably not high school and most definitely not middle school). And there are certainly plenty of helpful Christian books offering good advice on how to best develop a romantic relationship. This is not that book. This book is for the friends.

The author of the Book of Sirach in the Old Testament writes: "A faithful friend is a sturdy shelter: he that has found one has found a treasure. There is nothing so precious as a faithful friend, and no scales can measure his excellence; a faithful friend is an elixir of life; and those who fear the Lord will find Him" (Sirach 6:14–16). Another title for the Book of Sirach is "The Wisdom of Ben Sira," which feels very appropriate, because I can sense the deep wisdom in those words. True friends provide shelter within the storms of life. The value of friendship far surpasses that of material possessions, and so it is wise to seek out faithful friends. All of this is biblical truth. Here is another biblical truth: The Lord desires to give us friends. He does not wish for us to be alone. All we need to do is ask for that gift of faithful friendship, then get to work opening our arms to receive it.

1.

Why Your Friendships Desperately Need a Reset

As a young child, I cared about one thing: Sesame Place. You know the popular kids' TV show called *Sesame Street*? With Elmo and Oscar the Grouch and the Count and Big Bird? Truly iconic characters. Tragically, not enough people are aware that a Sesame Street-themed waterpark exists just an hour outside of Philadelphia and two hours outside of Manhattan. You heard that right. We all know about Disney World and Six Flags. Picture a smaller, less clean, cheaper version of those amusement parks—but Sesame Street themed. Imagine a Big Bird wave pool, a Cookie Monster splash pad, life-sized characters roaming the park poised to receive hugs and pose for priceless family pictures.

My family would visit this magical place once a year. That annual trip was the highlight of my existence, and I counted down the days until our Sesame Place excursion with greater devotion than I would for Christmas or my birthday. I was obsessed.

I vividly remember the morning of a Sesame Place outing when I was five years old. My family rose before the sun, and, bleary-eyed, we slurped orange juice and ate pancakes before piling into the minivan. The drive seemed to unspool in slow motion. To my five-year-old self, it felt like we hit every red light. Finally, my mom (who always drove while my dad helped with the maps) cruised into one of the massive parking lots near the entrance and I leapt out of the car. I was a sight: orange floaties clinging to my skinny arms, sunscreen slathered on my freckled face, and my heart beating so fast I felt like it was jumping out of my chest straight through my bathing suit. I couldn't wait for the day to begin.

After giving a quick high five to Bert and Ernie, the Craig family navigated the crowds toward the back of the park to the wave pool—the best part of any water park (this is not up for debate). We spread beach towels over lounge chairs and, as a group, trooped toward the water. As the chlorinated waves lapped over my toes, I gripped my dad's hand and positively vibrated with anticipation.

I peered up into his face. "Daddy?" I remember blurting out, my voice squeaky with excessive emotion.

"Yes, Maggie?" he asked, smiling down at me.

"Daddy, is heaven like Sesame Place?" Because in that golden moment, perfectly preserved in my memory, I could not imagine anything better. Nothing better than this.

With his characteristic kindness, Dad did not laugh at my ridiculous statement. Instead he gave my hand a gentle squeeze and said, "Oh sweetheart. Heaven is so much greater than this."

And it is.

I haven't been to heaven. You probably haven't either (if you have, please contact me because I have so many questions). But even though we have not been to heaven personally, someone we know has. Someone we trust. Someone we love.

That person is Jesus! Jesus knows heaven well. And what he has revealed to us about heaven through the Bible and through the private revelations of saints is that heaven is so much greater. So much greater than anything I could ever imagine.

Greater than the moment when my beloved Cleveland Cavaliers basketball team came back from a 3–1 deficit to triumph over the 73-win Golden State Warriors, claiming the 2016 NBA championship. Greater than my sister's wedding and the jubilant and raucous dance party afterwards. Greater than when I crossed the finish line at my first marathon. Greater than visiting Sesame Place as a five-year-old during a summer's afternoon in late August. Greater than *anything*.

That is our goal: heaven. As Christians, our purpose is not to just be a nice person. Is that important? Of course it is, but it isn't our only focus. The goal, the destination, the culmination of all our efforts is heaven. Heaven is not a physical location but rather a new state of being. Heaven is the eternal banquet feast of joy and peace with God and the community of believers (see Matthew 22:1–4). Heaven is the everlasting encounter with Jesus "face to face" (*Catechism of the Catholic Church*, 1023).

Studying abroad was a very popular option where I attended college. Students would take classes in Austria, the landlocked country in Europe and the location of one of my favorite movies of all time, *The Sound of Music*. Most would study in Austria for a semester during the spring of their sophomore year, or else in the fall of their junior year. I went to Europe the spring of my sophomore year (what a privilege; I am so grateful for the opportunity), while my best friend, Gabriela, sadly stayed back on main campus during that time. We were separated across an ocean for four months, and this was in the dark ages before smart phones and FaceTime. After the semester concluded, and I returned to the United States, Gabriela and I were apart for three more months over the summer. I worked as a camp counselor in Georgia, and she labored away at an internship at her home in the Midwest. Once the summer ended, and I came back to main campus for the start of my junior year, Gabriela went to Austria for four months. And then finally once she returned to the Land of the Free and the Home of the Brave, the Christmas season was upon us, and we were separated for another month over the break. That was a lot of time for us to be apart.

By the time the spring semester of our junior year began, both of us could hardly contain ourselves. We were finally back in the same zip code! The moment I arrived on campus, I punched Gabriela's number into my phone. I was pacing outside my dorm; she was renting textbooks from the library. We both ran to meet each other. When we saw each other, still over twenty yards away, we both screamed. We collided with the force of two 350-pound linebackers into a hug that still warms my heart as I think about it all these years later. Hands on each other's shoulders, we pulled out of the hug to look at each other face-to-face.

"Wow! I can't believe it's you!" I said.

"We're here! Reunited and it feels so good!" laughed Gabriela.

For all eternity, God has been waiting for our reunion. Of course, he is truly present to us here and now through sacred scripture, the sacraments, and his Body—the Church. But in a deeper, more mystical way, he is even more present to us in heaven. Heaven is the place of total union with God. A face-to-face encounter with our "Husband and Maker" (Isaiah 54:5), our "rock, fortress, and deliverer" (2 Samuel 22:2). Heaven is the goal. The wonderful and perfect reward that is waiting for us at the end of our earthly lives. No matter what is going on around us, we cannot lose sight of this goal.

Here is something that's not super fun to talk about: the devil is real. And he would love for us to lose sight of our heavenly goal. The devil is not a clownish red man carrying a pitchfork or other garden supplies. But there is a force in the world that is pulling us away from God and all that is good. Christians call that force the devil, or Satan, or Lucifer. We certainly do not have to be afraid of the devil, for God is so much more powerful. But we do have to be aware of how the evil one works. One of the ways the devil moves is that he tries to get us to grow complacent. He wants us to be lazy. He wants Christians to become unconcerned with our own habits and very concerned with the habits of others. Jesus warns us about this when he preaches: "Why do you see the speck that is in your brother's eye, but do not notice the log that is in your own eye?" (Matthew 7:3). What is Jesus saying here? Pay attention! Stop exclusively focusing on the faults of others and start focusing on improving your own!

We have faults. We are imperfect. We make bad decisions. We have sins and struggles and temptations. Unfortunately, I think that is something the modern mindset rejects. We like to pretend that there is nothing wrong with us and no matter what happens in our life or how we choose to act, we're completely fine and never to blame. But this is not true. This is not what Jesus teaches.

When I was a young kid, I had the idea that sin was just something for global terrorists or drug lords. I thought to myself: "I'm not a murderer, so I must not be a sinner." Congrats to thirteen-year-old Maggie! Even though I made the difficult decision not to become a contracted killer, I was still a sinner. I still am. St. Peter writes: "All have sinned and fall short of the glory of God" (Romans 3:23). No one is exempt! St. John echoes this: "If we say we have no sin, we deceive ourselves, and the truth is not in us" (1 John 1:8). We are all sinners. And yet, the Lord loves us anyway. He still chooses us and freely bestows his gifts upon us. Through the grace of God, heaven is a gift he wants to give us, but it is one we can never earn through our own merit. God is a merciful father who gives good gifts to us, his children (see Matthew 7:11). He gives us the gift of heaven, and he wants all of us to be saved so we can enter it with him (see 1 Timothy 2:4)! This is a free gift we do not deserve. But it's a gift we can choose to open. Through the way we live our lives, we can either accept this gift or reject it.

What must we do? We must examine ourselves. Fearlessly. We must look at our habits, studying every aspect of our lives with the courage to ask the questions: "Is my lifestyle directing me toward heaven? Are my hobbies drawing me closer to God? Is how I behave at my job helping me grow as a Christian? Are my academic habits leading me in the right direction? Are the movies I watch, music I listen to, books I read, social media I consume, and things I do on the weekend making me into the best possible version of myself right now and for eternity?" These questions are essential to ask. Here is another pivotal one: "Do my friendships point toward Christ?"

I'm noticing a self-improvement trend. Maybe it's not a trend, maybe it's a whole culture shift? I'm unsure what to call it. But whatever it is, it's happening. I see people, in person and in media and online, deciding to put in the work to improve their lives. 75 Hard, 75 Soft, Whole30, Exodus 90, half-marathon training regiments, protein intake, monitoring screen time, book clubs, accountability partners, cutting down or entirely eliminating alcohol and caffeine and sugar, and so on. It's impressive! I applaud it. I'm all for taking initiative and having the discipline to make positive changes. But I want these improvement efforts to expand to include something else: friendships.

I don't think we fully recognize the importance of friendships. Friendships have power, ultimate power! They can have sway over feelings and over actions. Think of the way you feel when your phone lights up with a text from someone you love. Think of the heavy weight that lodges in your stomach when you learn your coworkers went out to lunch without you. Think of the smile that spreads across your face when you remember the camping trip you took with your old college friends. Think of the way your heart drops when your buddy bails on you last minute, *again*. Think of the way your whole day brightens after your friend gives you a hug and looks you in the eye to ask how you are *really* doing.

When I was in graduate school, I rented out a house near campus with three other students. I barely knew them, but I was familiar with my roommate. Francesca and I shared a very small bedroom and an even smaller history. We had met years ago and had loosely hung out in similar friendship circles. But we never spent time together one-on-one before. I was hoping that would change once we were roommates and around each other all the time. That never happened.

Francesca was a nice person, but she was always absent. Physically and emotionally. Every Friday afternoon, she drove four hours home to visit her family and boyfriend and would not return until Monday afternoon. And when she was in town, we hardly saw each other. She stayed on campus late into the night and left early for her Dunkin' coffee fix before I even brushed my teeth. She wore headphones all day, so whenever we did see each other, she was listening to music on full volume or chatting with her boyfriend. She wrote essays in the living room sitting in front of the TV and wouldn't even look up when I walked through the front door. When we both cooked dinner at the same time, we mutely danced around each other, rummaging in the pantry for spices or opening the fridge without saying a single word.

I didn't need Francesca to be my best friend. Thankfully, I already had my network of supportive friends. I knew Francesca was about to graduate and was busy fulfilling all her requirements. I knew all these things. What I didn't know was why I was so sad. Why I felt like a dark cloud perpetually hovered over my street. Why I came up with excuses to delay going home. Why that semester was one of the worst in my entire academic experience. I didn't realize it at the time, but Francesca was deeply influencing me. I'm sure it was unintentional, but her indifferent behavior had a profound effect on my feelings.

That is what friends do: they affect us. That is the power they have.

Friends influence more than just our feelings. Their effect spills over into our actions. If your officemate starts going on walks during lunchtime, you will probably join him. If your teammate is obsessed with Harry Styles, and you sit with her on every bus ride to every game, you're probably going to start listening to his music too. If your friend group decides to watch every single Star Wars movie and TV show (including animated and live action, so we're talking hundreds of hours of content), most likely you're going to become invested in Star Wars lore. If your roommate starts smoking, there's a good chance you will pick up the habit. If your best friend joins a gym, you're more likely to get a membership.

One year when I was in college and had just come back to campus after the summer break, my friend Stephanie had picked up a new phrase none of us had heard before: "WOOF!" Stephanie used that word as an exclamation, sort of like a synonym for "WOW." After class, she would turn to me and say: "WOOF! That test was awful," or "WOOF! Did you see the sunset earlier? It was stunning!" or "WOOF! I only got thirty-two minutes of sleep last night. I'm exhausted." In less than a week, all my friends' vocabularies suddenly and prominently included the word "WOOF!" Me included!

I've heard it said that you are the average of the five people you spend the most time with. You absorb their terminology and habits, their outlook and decisions. You become a version of the people you surround yourself with. Can that be quantifiably tested? I don't know how, but looking back at my life, that statement feels pretty accurate.

Friendship has huge power over me.

And I know it's not just me.

Friendships have great influence over all our feelings and actions.

But it's more than just that.

At World Youth Day in 2004, Pope St. John Paul II declared to the millions of pilgrims gathered in Barcelona: "God uses human friendships to lead hearts to the source of divine charity." The Pope is telling us what we all know to be true, if we stopped to think about it. Friendships have power over our feelings and actions, absolutely. *And* friendships have the power to lead us to God. In a spiritually mysterious way, friendships directly influence our eternity.

The Gospel of Mark records a provocative story about this theme. Toward the beginning of his public ministry, Jesus is preaching in his hometown. So many townspeople are jammed into a house to listen to him speak that it's definitely a fire hazard. Four men, who are carrying a severely injured man on a mat, try getting close to Jesus but are unable to do so. There's no space for a single additional person. But they don't give up. Instead, they get creative. They scramble up on the roof. They make a hole through the tiles. They lower their paralyzed friend down through the ceiling to the feet of Jesus.

Jesus marvels at their determination: "And when Jesus saw their faith, he said to the paralytic, 'My sons, your sins are forgiven'" (Mark 2:5). Let's think about this for a second. Jesus forgives the sins of the paralytic and then later cures his injuries. He does this *not exclusively because of the man's own penitence*, but because of the faith of his friends. His friends! The actions of this man's friends led to his own physical and spiritual healing. Wow. What does that mean? Jesus is reinforcing the power of the people we surround ourselves with—they can even lead to our physical and spiritual healing.

We need to stop being so casual about our friendships and shift the way we see our friends. We cannot keep sliding into friendships like a cartoon character slides on a banana peel. We must intentionally select the people we spend time with, and we cannot afford otherwise. Too often, these are what our friendships look like:

Example #1: My mom's coworker gave birth around the same time as she did. My mom and her coworker wanted us, their kids, to be friends. Since Dave and I saw each other all the time growing up, we just sort of became best friends.

Example #2: Claire and I have been on the same traveling basketball team for the last five years. We see each other almost every day at practices and games and just sort of became best friends.

Example #3: Henry sat next to me on the first day of sixth grade. We have shared every class together since middle school and high school, and we just sort of became best friends.

Example #4: During high school and the summers between college, Sophie and I have worked at Dairy Queen. We have a ton of same shifts together, and we just sort of became best friends.

Example #5: Mike and I have lived in the same dormitory hall our entire college career. We have hung out almost every day for years and just sort of became best friends.

Example #6: My family and Heidi's family moved into the neighborhood around the same time. Every morning, we would see each other on our early morning walks with our kids in strollers. One day, we decided to stop waving to each other and actually go on walks together. We have been doing that for years and became really close.

Example #7: Dennis and I met in law school. We both didn't like studying alone, so we decided to study together almost every single day. All that time together led us to becoming best friends.

Example #8: I go to trivia on Wednesdays and began to recognize someone else who also participates every week. Marianne and I used to be fierce competitors, always battling it out for first or second place. Until one Wednesday when we decided to join forces and be on the same team. We dominated and have been best friends ever since.

There's nothing wrong with the origin stories of these friendships. I love hearing about them; they're great! The issue is not the beginning. Rather, the issue is the continuation without scrutiny, without stopping to question whether the friendship is aiding you in your quest for heaven.

You might say: "Maggie, calm down. I think you're being a little dramatic."

This might be true. I definitely am a dramatic person. Continue your accusation.

"As I was saying, Maggie, you're being extreme. Not every single friendship in my life has to be a direct elevator to heaven."

I agree with this. My mailman and I don't necessarily need to pray together every time he hands me a stack of junk mail. You and your older brother's long-distance girlfriend from Milwaukee don't need to have a Bible study together. It would be awesome if you did! But the effort to examine your friendships and begin improving them can be limited to those you spend the most time with. Identify your people. Your closest friends. Your inner circle.

Ask yourself: How healthy are my most cherished relationships? Are they oriented toward pursuing the good? Or are they more focused on accumulating the classic vices of wealth, power, and pleasure? Are my friends my "partners in crime," or are they fellow saints in the making? If you're unsure how to answer that question, make it even more basic: Are my friends people with good intentions? Do they love and respect their family and other friends? Do they treat their romantic partners well? How do they act toward their waiters and other members of the service industry? Do they care about the people around them or could they not care less? Do they cheat at school or at work or on their taxes? Is their speech affirming or degrading? Do they frequently gossip and easily lie? Do they keep their word and follow through? Are they the kind of people I want to be like?

As discussed, no one is a perfect person. Neither we nor our friends are flawless people. We all have flaws! The question is: Are our friends cooperating with the grace of God and actively working through their flaws? Or are they shrugging their shoulders and surrendering to the allurement of mediocrity, worldly pleasures, or bad behavior?

You might protest: "Well, Maggie, I don't know. My good friends are okay. I love them a ton, but we have our differences. They're not super moral or religious, but they're not horrible people. They're kind of neutral."

I understand why you might say that. I've said that about some of my friends before too!

Leah was one of my first actual friends. She had older siblings and seemed way more sophisticated than I was as a seventh grader. She fascinated me, and I found myself doing fun, new things with her that I had never done before. My parents didn't particularly like Leah. They didn't prevent me from hanging out with her, or stop her from coming over to our house, but they made their displeasure quietly known. They pointed out to me that Leah talked back to her parents, yelled at her siblings, and hid the truth about what she was doing. Before we'd leave her house, Leah would tell her mom we were going to the park. But then we would ride bikes to the thrift store instead. Or after we came back from getting ice cream, she'd tell her dad that we went to Subway.

"Do you really want to spend time with someone who acts that way, Maggie?" my mom would ask me as she drove me to school. I was a little uncomfortable about the whole situation, so I made excuses for Leah. I told my mom that she was just a little more edgy than me, but still a really great person. That Leah was working on being more honest and just had a strained relationship with her parents and siblings.

I defended her and praised her for some of her better qualities. "Leah is really smart, Mom. You should see her in class. And she's a great leader—she always takes charge and makes things happen. This was her first year on the soccer team, and she's improved so much! She's super fast and getting really good!" I watched Mom nod and purse her lips. I know now that my mother was letting me slowly realize what was so obvious to her all along.

As time went on, I noticed my own behavior start to shift. I found myself rolling my eyes at my parents, arguing with my sister more, and bending the truth about what I was actually up to. As if from a distance, I saw a change come over me, and I didn't like it.

Whenever I go to the movie theater, I always order a massive bag of popcorn. I know popcorn isn't the healthiest snack, but I also know it's not the worst for me. The moment I find my seat, I shovel popcorn into my mouth and devour the contents of the oversized bag. I'm enamored with the salty taste. Even though I know it's not the best, I love it, and it feels great as I eat it all. Until the movie ends and I walk out of the darkened theater into the dazzling sunlight.

My mouth feels gross. Dry. Stale. I guzzle water but can't wash out the taste.

That's how I began to feel about my friendship with Leah. I loved it at first. I thought Leah was a neutral kind of person. Maybe not the best for me, but certainly not the worst! I thought being friends with her would be fine. It felt exciting and special. Until I walked out into the sunlight and realized it had more of a negative effect on me than I thought. I'm sure Leah didn't mean to, but she was molding me into a version of herself. That's what all our friends do: raise us up to their level, or drag us down to meet them. There is no neutral.

What's a tree if it's not growing? Dead. The tree is either growing or dead. There is no in-between. The growth may not be incredibly obvious. It could be subtle. It may not be visible on the outside, but as long as positive movement is happening, the tree is alive.

There is no neutral in terms of friendships. The friendship is either helping you grow or helping you die. Bringing you closer to Jesus or dragging you away from him. This sounds kind of grim, but I believe it to be true. That's not to say you need to drop a friendship that isn't in peak health: it just means it needs extra attention. It needs a spring cleaning, a purification, a reorientation, a reexamination. It needs a reset.

2.

Lies About Friendship

I remember the scene perfectly.

The activity: Middle school dance.

The location: The cafeteria.

More precise location: Right by the water fountain next to the vending machines.

For the past hour, I had been dancing the only way I knew how: wildly. This meant I needed frequent hydration breaks. I exited the dance circle to slurp down some water from the dusty fountain. I was wiping the moisture off my mouth with the back of my hand when it happened. The first couple notes of a song thudded out of the DJ's speakers. The people around me screamed and immediately ran to the dance floor.

"What is this song?" I asked my classmates closest to me. I certainly was not an expert in pop music from the early to mid-2000s, but I recognized most of the songs playing that evening so far.

Mackenzie whipped her head around to stare at me, open mouthed: "You don't know this song?" she demanded with the ferocity of a police officer interrogating a mob boss.

I shrugged.

Mackenzie rolled her eyes. "I can't believe you don't know this song, Maggie. Everyone knows this song! We can't be friends." She threw her hands into the air and flounced back onto the dance floor.

Something changed in me in that moment. Underneath the flashing lights of a poorly funded junior high dance in northeast Ohio, I experienced an extremely powerful desire. The desire to be included. This was a brand-new feeling for me. I was definitely an odd ball growing up, and that didn't bother me at all. I was supremely unconcerned with what other people thought of me for my entire life, up until that particular instance. The only thing I cared about was having fun. Which to me looked like riding my scooter down the steepest sidewalks I could find, learning how to dribble a basketball between my legs, and trying to hold my breath underwater for as long as possible. I was never a loner. My exploits on the playground, at birthday parties, and on my sports team attracted some accomplices, but I never really considered them friends. And that was just fine with me. I cannot emphasize enough how little I cared about this. Until that exact moment. Until Mackenzie looked me up and down with the utmost scorn in that crowded cafeteria. After twelve years on earth, a fresh need began pumping through my bloodstream: the need to be included. And not just that: the need to have friends. And lots of them.

This catapulted me onto a grueling journey for many years, throughout the rest of my preteen and teenage years and into my early twenties. It's a tenuous thing, when you've convinced yourself that friendship is the main objective of your entire life. When you're consumed by it. When you're obsessed with accumulating relationships and maintaining them no matter the cost. When you place your whole identity entirely in your friends. For a solid amount of my life, I believed this commonly accepted lie that I like to call:

Lie #1 about Friendship: Friends are the *only* thing that matters.

Lie #1 is exhausting. You never stop, when you wholeheartedly believe that your entire self-worth is in the attention, affection, and affirmation of your friends. You're constantly performing. It's a never-ending tryout to qualify for the role of forever favorite. You need your friends to laugh at each joke you make. They have to choose to hang out with you every single weekend. You have to be picked first, preferred over everyone, adored nonstop. To accomplish this, you sacrifice a lot. Like your faith, your family, your hobbies, your peace. Not that those things aren't a big deal, they're just not as big of a deal as your friends. So, you push those things aside. You train yourself to become an Olympic gold medalist in social gymnastics, bending and twisting yourself to fit into the hearts of others. You need to be on that podium, and once you're there, you can't get off. There's no room for the real you when you believe your worth is rooted in what your friends think. I thought for so long that my authentic self, with all her quirks and insecurities, was nowhere near as desirable as the persona I constructed. For years I manipulated my personality and manufactured a character I would play as successfully as any Oscar-winning actress. All to chase the falsehood that friendship was the most important thing.

What does this lie look like in practice? I'll give you some hypothetical examples, which may or may not have come from my own life experience.

Example #1: Your family has a no-phone-past-8 p.m. policy, but you know your friend Ashley wants to talk to you about the new episodes of her favorite TV show. Even though you know you will get in trouble if caught, you sneak downstairs once your family is asleep and text Ashley late into the night.

Example #2: You have been assigned a group project with your friend Tyler. Tyler says he can't do any of the work because he's too stressed with his other assignments. You promise to help him out and complete the project by yourself.

Example #3: You sign up for your church's annual fall retreat, which is in two weeks. Your friend Matthew, who goes to another school, tells you about his high school's homecoming football game. He wants you to come with him, but it's the same weekend as the retreat. You back out of the retreat and go to the football game with Matthew.

Example #4: You and your sorority sister Olivia are enrolled in the same class, which has a strict attendance policy. Olivia wants to skip Friday's lecture to go visit her boyfriend out of state. She asks you to cover for her by checking off her name on the attendance sheet that is passed around at the beginning of every class. When the attendance sheet is handed to you, you cross off your own name as well as Olivia's.

Example #5: Spring break is approaching, and you decide to go on a mission trip during your time off from school. You start fundraising and attending meetings with the rest of the people who will be going on the mission. A week before spring break, you run into your buddy Kyle outside of the library. He tells you that he and a few friends are going rock climbing out in Colorado over the break. They have one open seat in their car and are looking for an extra person to help split the costs. You tell them you're in.

Example #6: Over the Christmas break, you and your friends sign up to take snowboarding lessons. The day before your first lesson, your friends decide they would rather learn to ski instead and ask you to drop snowboarding to be with them. You have always dreamed of learning to snowboard, and you already know how to ski. You agree and join them anyways.

Example #7: Even though you're of age and drinking is completely legal, you decide to take a break from alcohol. Your coworkers have a weekly Wednesday happy hour at a nearby restaurant. You don't quite trust yourself to be in an environment with a lot of alcohol right now, so you decide not to join them until you feel strong enough. On Wednesday during lunch, your coworkers ask if you're coming with them for drinks after work. You hesitate. "Come on!" they beg. You relent.

Example #8: You have accepted a new job in a new city. Your position requires you interact with people all day, which is a challenge for you because you're an introvert. You are looking to rent a one-bedroom apartment so you can recharge after work. You tell your friend Austin about your move. He is thrilled for you and has some news of his own. He just found out his job is transferring him to the same city where you're moving. He asks if you two can look for an apartment to rent out together. You agree.

The reality is that this kind of decision-making can only go on for so long. Something will happen to force you to open your eyes. A friend moves away and your phone calls dwindle. You change classes or schools or majors and don't see your friends as much. A new person enters the friend group and shifts the dynamic. You discover you disagree with your friend on a significant moral issue. Your friend hurts your feelings for the tenth time, and you realize you can't hold back your tears until you are in the safety of your own room. You get a promotion, and your friend does not, so he avoids you for a week. You get cut from the basketball team while your friend is still on varsity. Your friend laughs at a cruel joke made by another one of your friends, and you realize you have been sacrificing so much of your time and energy for people you don't even like. And who might not even like you that much either.

This realization will come. The realization that you elevated your friendships far higher than what is healthy. That you rested your whole weight on something that was never designed to hold you. This discovery can happen quickly. Like a light switch flipped on and all of a sudden you're awake. Something specific happens, and you look at your friends and you look at yourself and all at once, you can't understand why you acted this way for so long. Or the revelation can grow slowly, like a sunrise. The light leaks through the clouds almost imperceptibly until it takes over and you can't believe there was a time you didn't see it.

For me, it was the sunset route. Growing in relationship with God made me realize how toxic my own earthly relationships had become. It wasn't even necessarily my friendships that were unhealthy; it was me and my own expectations of them. Ideally, friendships reveal God, and they can lead you to God. But they are *not God*. They reflect the Divine—they are not the Divine himself. Jesus invites: "Come to me, all who labor and are heavy laden and I will give you rest" (Matthew 11:28). Finding rest in God taught me to properly order what I let become disordered. When I began to understand that he alone satisfies me, I stopped expecting my friends to fill a void they were never meant to. After much heartache, I began the process of rooting my identity in the Creator, not in his creatures.

Let me tell you: I am *not* perfect at this! There have been *many* times in my life when I let **Lie #1** slither back into my outlook and behavior. Thankfully, Jesus is patient and constant. He is a gentle gardener always read to prune what does not bear fruit in me (see John 15:2). The key is sticking close to Jesus. If we remain focused on worshipping him alone, we will stop idolizing anything or anyone else. Then we can truly love our friends for who they are: companions on the journey to God, not God himself.

Lie #2 about Friendship: Friends do *not* matter.

This lie is on the opposite end of the spectrum. Where **Lie #1** prizes friendship above anything else, **Lie #2** places too little value on friendship. On the list of personal priorities, **Lie #2** either puts friends on the bottom or takes them off the list entirely. **Lie #1** encourages you to exert way too much effort on friendship. **Lie #2** discourages you from exerting any sort of effort at all.

Bethany and I met in college when we were camp counselors at a Christian summer camp. By the time our friendship was starting to take off, the summer ended, and we went back to our different hometowns and colleges. Even though we were physically separated by time zones and state lines, Bethany and I kept growing in friendship. We spent hours on the phone together, chatting as I drove to my internship and she cooked dinner, while I went on walks around my neighborhood and she rode the train downtown.

This long-distance friendship was really fun and brought a lot of joy to both of our lives. But it also forced us both to do something new: put effort into our friendships. We didn't really know that was a thing. We thought friendships naturally unfolded and just sort of happened. We began to realize that if we wanted this friendship to stick around in a meaningful way, we had to put in the work!

That started with communication. All we could do was talk! It wasn't like we could go to the movies or get froyo together or do any of the other things that friends do when they see each other regularly. Talking was the only option, and we talked a lot. We figured out how to have difficult conversations, how to tell the truth while also being kind, how to handle differences in outlook, how to apologize and to forgive each other when one of us said something hurtful. We learned all about each other and gained some valuable tools in our friendship toolbox in the process. We have now been friends for over a decade, and I know one of the main reasons our friendship is still so strong is because we both realized that the other person is worth it. Friendship is worth it.

A year or so ago, Bethany and I were having dinner with some of our other friends. I can't remember the exact context, but we were talking intensely about something that was really important to both of us. We weren't even close to arguing, but we were serious and speaking directly, communicating our feelings clearly. Later that evening when Bethany was on the other side of the room, my friend Riley turned to me: "Maggie," she asked, eyes wide. "Be real with me. How often do you and Bethany have hard conversations?"

I frowned, thinking. "I'm not sure. Probably every day. Why?"

Riley blinked. "I don't think I've ever had a serious conversation like that with my friends before."

"Oh," I said. "Well, I recommend it!"

Riley is not to blame here. She, like so many people, did not fully understand that the healthiest friendships require effort. This is a totally foreign concept to so many people. And I don't have to wonder why. No one is talking about how to be a good friend! Turn on the radio: almost every single song is a romantic love song. Go to the movies: almost every single film is about, or heavily features, a love story. Walk into the teenage or young adult or adult section of your local bookstore: almost every single book is about, or heavily features, romance. Friends certainly appear in entertainment, but usually only as subplots. They are typically one-dimensional characters who are used to add humor or inspiration or distraction from heartbreak. They roll into their friend's life like a tumbleweed and stick around no matter how much they're neglected once the romance resumes.

The world places huge value on romantic relationships over almost anything else. Media loves narratives on how to be attractive, how to be a good partner, how to be a good spouse. Meanwhile, no one is talking about how to be a good friend. We know other relationships involve working through struggles. We know that communication and honesty and energy are necessary in family relationships and with a romantic partner. We know that. But for some reason, we think those things are not necessary in platonic relationships. This mindset is incredibly harmful and a setup for friendship failure. Without time and effort dedicated to developing actually healthy and meaningful friendships, guess what? We are not going to have healthy and meaningful friends! We are going to be left with weak platonic bonds—paper-thin relationships that are way closer to acquaintances than they are to substantial friendships.

I don't mean to brag (I do), but there was a time in my life when I could bench press. Not a ton of weight, but I could confidently pump out some reps. What I knew about lifting weights was that I wanted to lift the heavy ones and lift them a lot. I knew that maintaining proper form was essential, but I also knew I had to keep going when I felt the burn—especially when I felt the burn. You don't stop when you feel the burn. The burn is good! It's how the body develops muscle! No resistance equates to no strength gains. Just like in lifting weights, healthy friendships are going to encounter resistance. That is okay! As long as we maintain the proper form of keeping God first and foremost, we don't have to be afraid of any conflict we might encounter in our friendships.

It is possible that believing **Lie #2** can be more expansive. Embracing this lie could apply to other relationships too. Or *all* relationships. I know these people. You know these people! Maybe you have been this person before, like I have been at times in my life. Some people have convinced themselves that they don't need anyone else. All they need is themselves, and that is the only relationship they focus on. They shut themselves down and close themselves off. They might describe themselves as a lone wolf. An extreme introvert. Someone with social anxiety. Someone who prefers to live "without drama" that comes from relationships. Someone who says friendships are a waste of time. Someone who is entirely occupied with their career or academics or fitness or hobbies. Someone who claims that they just do not have the time or willpower to bother with friends.

I'm not knocking introverts or people who have social anxiety. I absolutely believe in those things and know they are real and valid. I also think that focusing on your career and school and hobbies are worthy things to do. But none of these things are legitimate reasons to ignore friendships. We cannot use them as shields for emotional intimacy. I have so much empathy for people who believe **Lie #2**, especially in this iteration of it, as they have often been wounded in ways they do not deserve. **Lie #2** is a defense mechanism, a desperate attempt to cover up pain and to prevent future hurt. I understand it, but I don't endorse it—because I know it doesn't lead to fulfillment.

Genesis, the first book of the Bible, is many things, but it is not an academic textbook. It does not teach scientific truths about *how* human beings were created. Rather, it teaches *why* we are created. We are created to bear the image and likeness of God (Genesis 1:27). In Genesis, God begins the human race with Adam. I love imagining Adam in the Garden of Eden before the arrival of Eve. Adam was living the true bachelor life, roaming around the garden, buck naked, hanging with all the animals. In many ways, it seemed like everything should have been perfect for him. But it was not. God looked at Adam and realized Adam was missing something. He was missing someone. He was lonely.

God's first assessment of human nature is: "It is not good that the man should be alone" (Genesis 2:18). The Triune God's earliest observations of humans is not that we need more discipline, extra sleep, or stronger deodorant. What we need is each other. In the earliest chapters of the Sacred Book for both Jewish people and Christians alike is the declaration that relationships matter. What is true for Adam is true for all of us. Adam needed someone else and we do too. It is not good for us to be alone.

Will we experience seasons of loneliness? Certainly, and that is completely normal. Should we seek out solitude to communicate with God in the silence of our hearts? Yes and amen. But our permanent state must be one of communion with others. You might be going through a move, a time of transition, a quarter-life crisis, or a global pandemic. You still need friendships. It doesn't matter if you're an introvert or extrovert or anything in between. How you get your energy doesn't impact this reality. Regardless of personality type, Myers-Briggs, enneagram, or any other form of self-categorization, there can be no disqualification from the fact that God made humans to be in relationship with one another. Even if God gifted you with a special vocation as a female or male religious in a cloistered convent or hermitage, you would still live in community with your religious brothers or sisters. There is no exception.

What does believing in Lie #2 practically look like? Again, I will provide some potentially hypothetical examples, which may or may not have come from my own life experience.

Example #1: Your family moves to a new city for the fourth time in two years. On your first day of school, you choose a seat in the back of every class, away from everyone else. You avoid the cafeteria at lunch time, sit by yourself at study hall, and do not talk to your classmates as you leave school at the end of the day. You are confident that your family will move again soon and it is not worth it to get to know new people.

Example #2: Your high school hosts its annual Winter Carnival in January, a snow-themed festival with hot chocolate, sledding, and snowball fights. Every year, you spend the day with the friends that you met at your first winter carnival when you were a freshman. But this year you have a crush on a girl in your Spanish class and think Winter Carnival would be a great opportunity to get to know her better. You tell your friends you will not be able to hang with them this time because you will be with someone else.

Example #3: You have been tight with Carter since elementary school, but you are both going to different colleges soon. You know you're not going to see Carter as much anymore, so you don't bother spending time with him over the summer or responding to his texts.

Example #4: Your family has been close with your neighbors your whole life. The youngest neighbor is getting married June 15th. You eagerly RSVP *yes*. A week and a half before the wedding, your girlfriend tells you that her cousin (whom you have never met) is also getting married on June 15th, but several states away. She wants you to join her as her date to her cousin's wedding. You tell your neighbor you can't come anymore and you attend your girlfriend's cousin's wedding instead.

Example #5: You enroll in a university far away from home where you don't know anyone else. Once you arrive on campus, you decide to skip orientation and other new student activities. You don't visit the club fair, nor do you sign up for any organizations or volunteer groups. You decide it's better to just focus on your academics and not waste your time with any social distractions.

Example #6: You and your college roommate didn't know each other before you moved in, but in the first couple weeks of the semester you have become pretty good friends. You have a couple of the same classes, and afterward you enjoy playing video games together in your room. One day, you notice that some of the snacks and drinks you keep in your mini fridge are missing. You restock, and the next week you notice that they're running low. Your roommate has to be responsible. Instead of directly addressing him, you decide it would just be easier to move out. You meet with your RA and request a roommate transfer.

Example #7: Your friend Carmen's birthday party is the last Saturday of the month. You already bought decorations, and you're looking forward to getting together. Two days before the party, your boyfriend tells you he got offered an exciting work opportunity. But it involves him traveling out of the country for a few weeks. He wants to spend the whole weekend with you before he leaves, but Carmen's birthday is on Saturday. You decide time with your boyfriend is more important, so you text Carmen and apologize that you won't be able to make her birthday.

Example #8: You became friends with Will through work. For the past couple months, you have been scheduled for the same shift and have had a great time working together. You often hang around after work ends, talking in the break room. Will suggests getting coffee together sometime on your day off and you're all in. You just received your new work schedule and see that you and Will aren't working the same shifts anymore, which means you probably won't see each other as much. You think about texting Will and asking him about getting coffee, but decide against it.

Solo time and time spent with your boyfriend/girlfriend/spouse has its time and place, but we need friendships. There is no substitute. There is no getting around this. Constantly being alone or spending time only with your significant other will not satisfy you in the way that friendships do. Does that mean we have to be popular? Absolutely not. It's pointless and unhealthy to chase mass approval. Not even Jesus was unanimously popular! He was literally tortured to death at the encouragement of people worshipping him less than a week previously. It's foolish to pursue the fiction of universal admiration. What should we focus on instead? Rejecting **Lie #2** and working to develop a strong network of trusted friends.

3.

Friendship Red Flags

I grew up in Ohio, but I was born in New Jersey (two very under-appreciated states). My family would often return to New Jersey in the summers to visit our old friends and spend time at the beach. I loved when my family did this, but the summer I turned thirteen, I was not too enthusiastic. I was going through some friendship drama that was distracting me from the sunshine and Italian ice. Instead of riding bikes down to the shore with my family and our friends one afternoon, I hung back at the house and hung over my phone. My Nokia 2000 lit up with text after text from Alyssa, one of my best friends at the time. We were fighting, which seemed to be something we were doing a lot of that summer. I missed her birthday party, she skipped my bonfire, and the reality that we were going to different schools the next month loomed heavy over our heads. And the biggest issue of all, my parents didn't seem to like her that much (parents always know). Her texts were long, scathing, and coming in fast. I leaned my head on the counter and began to cry.

I didn't notice my dad pushing open the screen door until he rested his hand on the crown of my head. My dad, a father of girls, was unfazed by tears: "Is this about Alyssa?" he gently asked. I looked up at him and sniffed in response.

"You know, Maggie," he said, lightly stroking my hair, "friends are supposed to give you wings. Not chains. And it doesn't seem like you're soaring."

"Okay, Yoda," I muttered. But I leaned over and let Dad circle his arms around me. The truth rolled over me like the nearby waves. I knew he was right.

I don't know if Dad came up with this adage or not, but I give him full credit. This statement has fruitfully guided my approach to friendships ever since. I have learned that nostalgia is not a good enough reason to continue being friends with someone. Neither are inside jokes, common interests, or convenience. Regardless of shared history, if a friendship is chaining you down in any way, it has to be worked on.

What do I mean by "chained down"? This is a process, a slow buildup of little things that accumulate into really big things. Here are some issues to look for in a friendship that desperately needs to be reset:

Issue #1 You don't feel like your true self: you feel you have to minimize or discredit things that are important to you, like your faith or interests or other friendships.

Issue #2 You don't feel like your best self: you feel pressured into doing things you know you shouldn't, or into *not* doing things you know you should.

Issue #3 You feel like you can't be honest: your opinions are disregarded or ridiculed.

Issue #4 You don't feel valued: through things said or unsaid, done or not done, you just aren't being treated kindly.

Here are some concrete examples of these red flags:

Example #1: You and your friends go to the movie theater. After the movie ends, you all get burgers and share your thoughts about the film. "I can see how the movie was objectively good, but I personally didn't like it that much," you tell your friends in between bites of your french fries. "It was a little too gory and violent for me."

Madison rolls her eyes. "Of course you would say that!" she says to the group. "You are such a baby, and you don't even have that much cinema literacy to understand the significance."

Example #2: You have an exam on Friday morning that acts as a large percentage of your overall grade. Your plan is to spend as much time as you can on Thursday studying in the library. At breakfast on Thursday morning, your friend Max comes up to you and tells you that he has an extra ticket to a concert that night. He invites you to join. You tell him, "I would love to go! Thank you for the invite, but I have a huge test tomorrow and need to study all day today." Max scoffs. "You're always like this! You used to be so much more fun and now you're hyper-focused on academics. You worry too much about school. Come to the concert." You tell Max you want to, but you can't. Max mutters something under his breath and storms off.

Example #3: You sign up to run your first half-marathon. You're nervous but also really excited. Over dinner, you tell your friends the news. All of them are thrilled for you, except Kayla. "I don't know if that's a good idea, Maggie," Kayla says. "I ran a half-marathon a couple years ago and it was super hard for me. And I was in really good shape. And, no offense, but you just don't have a runner's body. Is it too late to back out?"

Example #4: You walk into the break room to have lunch with some of your coworkers. Before you take a bite of your sandwich, you take a second and offer up a silent prayer. You thank God for the gift of your food and ask his special grace on all those who go without. As you begin chewing on your tuna sandwich, one of your coworkers turns to you and asks: "Why are you always doing that?"

You swallow before asking, "Doing what?"

"Why do you close your eyes before you eat?" Cory says.

"Oh!" You explain: "I pray before every meal."

Cory makes a face. "Why?"

"Because I'm a Christian. I pray throughout my day, and before I eat is a great time to do so. It's also a privilege to have food and I'm grateful for that."

Cory stares at you for a second. "That seems kind of ridiculous to me," he says before returning back to his salad.

Example #5: Your New Year's resolution is to become more financially responsible. You have paid off some debt and made a lot of progress, but you still have a long way to go. Your friend calls to share the news that she got a promotion and wants to go out to celebrate. You congratulate her but are unsure of what she means by "celebrate." She tells you she wants to get dinner and drinks at a new restaurant downtown. You hesitate. "Kathleen, I am so proud of you. You deserve to be celebrated! But I don't have the money right now to get dinner and drinks. I would love for you to come over this weekend, though! We can make our own drinks at home and you can tell me all about your new responsibilities at work."

Kathleen is silent for a moment, then says: "Why can't you be more supportive of me? You know how hard I work at this job. I know your job is rough right now, but I thought you of all people would be excited for me." She then hangs up.

Example #6: Your group of friends gets tickets to a baseball game in another city. You decide to make a weekend trip out of it and are having a great time brainstorming what all you're going to do. You tell your friends, "Just so you know, I'm going to go to church on Sunday. It's totally fine if I go by myself and I can meet up with you all later, but just a heads up about what I'm going to do." Jack is not a fan of that plan. "But we're on vacation! In a brand-new city! You can go to church when you're back home."

You say to Jack: "Going to church is important to me, even when I'm on vacation. But I can figure out how to get myself there and back and you all can do whatever you want during that time."

Jack huffs. "I feel like that's pretty pretentious of you. You pray enough already."

Example #7: You and your friend Christina have been so busy that you haven't seen each other recently. You decide to spend time together next Friday and are coming up with ideas of what to do. "We could order Indian food and watch that new TV show that just came out," you suggest. "I've had a pretty stressful week and that sounds really relaxing."

"Isn't that a kids' show?" Christina asks.

"Well, not really," you say. "I hear it's good and I definitely want to watch it."

Christina barks out a laugh through the phone. "What kind of adult likes stuff like that? You're into such weird things. We should do something else that's actually fun."

Example #8: You have been feeling kind of sluggish lately. You decide to go outside your comfort zone and join a new gym. Your first weight lifting class is on Tuesday. The next time you see your friend Jacob, you tell him about this new thing you're trying out. Since he's really into fitness, you figured that Jacob would be excited. "Hey Jacob, guess what? I'm finally going to exercise more. I joined a gym and a weight lifting class this week!" Jacob raises his eyebrows.

"What?" you ask him.

"Are you sure you can handle that kind of commitment?" Jacob says.

"What do you mean?"

"Well," he rubs his hand through his hair. "You're not the most consistent person out there. You often flake on plans. You need to be serious about this and I don't think you're there yet."

We all deserve love, in every aspect of our lives. But especially in our friendships. St. Thomas Aquinas reasoned that to love means to choose and to will the good of the other. Examine your friendships, or one relationship specifically. Is this friend truly loving you? They don't have to be perfect. They will not be perfect! And neither will you. But the effort has to be there. The majority of the time, is this friend actually choosing, willing, and helping you seek what is good in your life? If any part of you doesn't think so, don't ignore that.

Friends are not just people you spend time with because you have nothing else better to do. Friends are not just people who have the same sense of humor as you. Friends are not just people who like the same TV shows as you. Friends are not just people who have the same hobbies as you. Real friends are so much more than that. Friendships are meant to be this energy bank of support and encouragement and praise. When you're plugged into your healthy friendships, through the grace of God you become the best possible version of yourself. Friends are meant to love you and join you on your journey to becoming a saint. Anything less than that is not acceptable. Jesus is the way, the truth, and the life (John 14:6). Recognize the truth that you deserve more.

What are you to do? How do you reset what has grown stagnant? Here is what you need:

Reset Tool #1: Prayer.

Prayer is crucial to the life of the Christian. Nonnegotiable. Prayer is not *part* of your relationship with God—it *is* your relationship with God. If we are not prioritizing prayer, we are not prioritizing God or our faith. We don't have to commit to hours of silent prayer on our knees throughout the night. But we do have to make it part of our daily life in an achievable and consistent way. And we have to incorporate prayer into our friendships. We need to invite God into this process of purification. Jesus loves to heal! While on earth, he spent years traveling around healing all who asked. He will do the same for you. Ask God for help. Study the scriptures, receive the sacraments, serve the poor, spend time in silence. And as you do so, carry this intention within your heart: "Lord Jesus, please heal my friendships."

Prayer Example #1: You are about to visit the farmer's market with a friend you haven't seen in a while. You're a little anxious about spending time together since it's been so long. In the car before you drive to the farmer's market, you take a second to say a prayer. To ask God for courage. For him to make you a vessel of his peace.

Prayer Example #2: Your friend Lily's favorite food is Honeycrisp apples. Every time you see an apple, either at the store or at a restaurant, you think of Lily. You take that reminder as an opportunity to pray for her. You lift her and her intentions up to the Lord and ask that he bless her.

Prayer Example #3: You know that you're supposed to brush your teeth for two minutes at a time to get them thoroughly clean. During those two minutes, you decide to take a break from scrolling on your phone. Instead, you use that short time to pray for your basketball team during their upcoming season. You ask God to keep the players and coaches safe from injury and to remain focused on him in all things.

Reset Tool #2: Bravery.

This whole situation of assessing your friendships is definitely scary. It would be so much easier to put your head down and ignore the warning signs and go on being unhappy in your friendships. Rocking the boat takes guts, but sometimes the boat has to be rocked to get it going in the right direction again. The most frequent command in scripture is: "Do not be afraid." Versions of that statement are found 365 times in the Bible. One reminder for every day of the year (except leap year—be afraid on that day). God constantly reminds us to have courage, and we especially need it here. No matter what happens, we have to be brave. If our friends accept this change or if they reject it, we must "put on the Lord Jesus Christ" and the courage that comes from him (Romans 13:14).

Bravery Example #1: As an extrovert, you almost always feel energized after spending time with people. But after hanging out with your friend Ava for the last couple weeks, you have felt drained and tense. Ava has been your friend for years and has supported you through some tough times. You are so grateful for her friendship and are tempted to just push past your recent anxieties. But you know you need to have a conversation. You get your phone and message Ava, asking if you can call her to talk to her about something.

Bravery Example #2: A few years ago, you met Noah at church. You are part of the same Bible study and small group and have become good friends. But recently, Noah has stopped coming to small group and Bible study and rarely goes to church anymore. You miss him. When you ask Noah where he's been, he gets angry. He tells you he's not sure what he believes anymore. He says he feels judged by you and that he would rather spend his Sundays mountain biking in nature. Part of you wants to shrug your shoulders and just let your friendship with Noah fall apart–that would definitely be easier and stop Noah from being mad at you. But you know you owe it to yourself and him to try to talk through this. You text Noah and ask if you can join him on a mountain biking ride on Saturday so you can bring this up with him.

Bravery Example #3: You and Emma have been playing basketball together since you were five and have been great friends ever since. You are both the youngest players on your varsity basketball team. Over the summer, Emma has been training with some of the seniors and hanging out with them after practice. Now at the start of the school year, you and Emma have been spending less time together because she is with the older players more and more. Emma has been going to parties with the seniors, sneaking out, and not telling her parents where she really is. Emma is also acting differently toward you. She is way more serious and now has a biting, sarcastic sense of humor. This is starting to affect your friendship. You care about Emma but know she will not like what you want to say to her. You're afraid that if you talk to Emma about this, it might cost you your friendship. Yet you know you need to. After practice, you approach Emma and ask if you can walk back to the training room with her to talk about something.

Reset Tool #3: Discernment.

Discernment is a fancy religious term that means having our eyes and ears open to what is going on around us physically and spiritually. Pope Francis says that discernment "requires that I know myself, that I know what is good for me here and now. Above all, it requires a filial [close, loving, etc.] relationship with God" (General Audience, August 31, 2022). Through the direction of the Holy Spirit, discernment allows us to honestly assess our friendships. To recognize friction. To concretely identify what is going on. To peacefully acknowledge the specific issues and then have the conviction to do something about it.

Discernment Example #1: "My friendship with Matt feels like it's going through a rough patch. It probably stems from the fact that I'm noticing Matt making fun of me in front of other people. His comments make me feel small and unimportant."

Discernment Example #2: "Why has my friendship with Hannah been making me upset? Most likely it's because Hannah has started dating someone a few years older than her. She now spends almost all her time with her new boyfriend and his friends, rather than with me and our group of friends. I'm feeling left behind and I want my friends to see me as a priority."

Discernment Example #3: "Things with Jimmy have been challenging recently. On the surface, it doesn't look like there's anything wrong. But he has raised his voice at me more than a few times when we're just talking about random things. He plays it off as a joke, but it doesn't feel funny to me. I want to stay friends with Jimmy, but I don't like being yelled at and I want him to treat me better."

Discernment Example #4: "Ever since I went back to school after Christmas break, I have had a hard time sleeping and can't seem to focus while doing my homework. I tried to just get over it, but I'm constantly overwhelmed. My new class schedule is really demanding and because of that, I haven't spent as much time connecting with Jesus through prayer or hanging out with my friends."

Without discernment, red flags seem gray and vague. You can't fix a problem you don't see. God is all about light. His first recorded words are, "Let there be light!" (Genesis 1:3), and Jesus describes himself as "the light of the world" (John 8:12). He restores sight to the blind, and when he calls his first apostles, he tells them: "Come and see" (John 1:39). God wants us to see! We won't have perfect spiritual vision on earth, but God doesn't want us to be blind. Discernment helps remove the blindfold in all aspects of life, and friendship is no exception.

Reset Tool #4: Vulnerability.

To be vulnerable is to be humble enough to expose your heart to another person. Vulnerability says, "This is where I hurt, this is where I am ashamed, these are the parts of me I would rather hide, but I am choosing to share them with you." Vulnerability is an emotional exposure. An uncovering of a weakness or hidden pain. Intimidating, but essential.

One day when I was around ten years old, I was happily swinging on a giant rope swing. The backyard of my childhood home opened up to a forest, and several years previously, my dad climbed up an oak tree and set up the perfect swing. On this September evening, catastrophe struck. A stray tree branch snagged my right leg a few inches above my ankle and pulled back the skin to reveal the bone. As fast as I could, I hobbled home. My mom took one look then ordered me into the car. As we sped off toward the hospital, she frantically prayed for all green lights, and I examined a *Where's Waldo?* book in a daze. We arrived at the emergency room, and the doctors sewed up my right leg with thirty-seven stitches. The wound is still visible on my leg to this day.

Before we left the hospital, a doctor assured me I would recover just fine. All I had to do was let one of my parents rub some special ointment on my wound twice a day, once in the morning and once at night. After the ointment was smeared onto my leg, Mom or Dad would tightly wrap a bandage over the wound. The tightness would help me feel secure. As long as I took it slow, I could carefully limp around and avoid relying on the dreaded crutches, a nemesis for anyone who lives in an icy area. No one would know about my wound, for it would be concealed by the bandage. At the end of the day, my parents would unwrap the bandage, rub the medicine onto the stitched skin, and wrap it back up before I drifted off to sleep.

That is exactly what my parents and I did for months: unwrap bandage, ointment on, tightly wrap bandage, repeat. I kept my wound a secret. The tale certainly would have captivated my wide-eyed classmates and earned me an awed form of respect for visiting such an exotic place as the emergency room. But I kept the information to myself. I knew the injury was my own fault, and I was ashamed of the wound hidden underneath the bandage.

After several months, the routine suddenly changed. On a Tuesday night before bed, my mom removed the bandage and rubbed the ointment onto the wound as she always did. But then that was it. She hugged me goodnight and stood up to leave the room before I called her back.

"Mom, what are you doing?" I gestured forcefully to my leg. "You didn't wrap the bandage around my wound."

Leaning against my doorframe, Mom smiled down at me. "Honey, it's time."

"Time?" I retorted. "It's time to call Child Protective Services. Take care of me! Wrap up my wound!"

Mom sighed. "Maggie, it's time. If you keep your wound wrapped up any longer, it will get infected and never heal."

She of course was right. I had reached the point where I had to change. I couldn't hide my wound anymore. If I tried to do so, the wound would fester. It would begin to rot, and it certainly wouldn't recover. I needed to take off the bandage and expose my wound to the air and light in order to heal.

All of us have wounds. Some of us do physically, but I'm speaking here of emotional wounds. Some wounds are given to us by other people: generational trauma or violence committed against us at the hands of strangers or those who should have cared for us most. Other wounds are self-inflicted, pain we have given to ourselves through our own sin, destructive habits, or indifference.

All of us have wounds and almost all of us prefer to keep them hidden. We limp through life and shrug off our pain. We don't want to tell anyone. We bury our wounds under layers of fear or denial, confident that they will be used against us if exposed. We're positive that, if our wounds are brought to light, we will be rejected, humiliated, and banished from our relationships, as well as disqualified from our responsibilities. Meanwhile our wounds just get worse.

My mom knew what to do. "It's time," she told me. And I tell you the same. It's time to expose your wounds—first, to Jesus Christ the Divine Healer, who declared in Luke's Gospel: "Those who are well have no need of a physician, but those who are sick. I have not come to call the righteous, but sinners to repentance" (Luke 5:31–32). God is not repulsed or intimidated by the damage sin has done to our hearts. Rather, Jesus the Savior is eager to save. The God who created the universe can and will create you anew, if you are vulnerable to him and expose your wounds to his divine healing (Revelation 21:5).

The Lord invites us to be vulnerable with him, but also to be vulnerable with our trusted friends. Too often we adopt a posture of indestructability within friendships. We pretend with ourselves and others that we have no struggles, no issues, no heartache, no reason to suspect we aren't as perfect as we claim. Nothing bothers us, nothing ruffles us. We are chill, self-sufficient, and just fine.

But this mirage of flawlessness doesn't help anything, let alone our friendships. We must abandon the act and admit to God, ourselves, and our close friends that we have wounds. This vulnerability leads to deeper intimacy. Our friends will know us better, and the better you know someone, the better you can love them. Vulnerability brings closeness, as well as support. When our friends know our wounds, they can look out for us in a unique way. The examples below are possible responses to the Discernment Examples on pages 42 and 43:

Vulnerability Example #1: "Matt, I was bullied a lot when I was younger. It was awful and I never want to go through that again. I don't want to be bullied in my friendships. I don't think you do it on purpose, but sometimes I feel like the butt of a joke to you, and I really don't like feeling that way. I want to laugh and have fun with you, but I don't want you to make fun of me. Can you help me with this?"

Vulnerability Example #2: "Hannah, I miss spending quality time with you. Ever since you started dating your new boyfriend, I've felt left out. I've had friends choose their boyfriends over me in the past, and it makes me feel replaceable. I know you don't mean to make me feel this way, but it makes me feel like you don't really care about me anymore. Can you help me with this?"

Vulnerability Example #3: "Jimmy, you are one of my closest friends, and I'm so grateful for you in my life. But recently I've been feeling some tension and aggression from you. Last week when we were watching hockey at your house, you raised your voice at me. And a few days before that, you yelled at me when we were driving to school. I haven't told you this before, but while my parents were separating, my dad was verbally and physically aggressive with me. It has taken me a while to work through that pain, and when you yell at me, everything resurfaces. Can you help me with this?"

Vulnerability Example #4: "Eve, I'm wondering if you can help me. Ever since this semester started, I have been feeling really anxious and removed from my friends and from God, partly because of my class load. Would you be able to go to Mass with me once a week and then study together afterward? That way I can make sure I have God time and friend time while still getting work done."

Vulnerability might steer your relationship into unchartered territory. Maybe you have never been this serious with your friend before. They may be startled by your disclosure, and it might take them some time to process your vulnerability. This is all totally understandable. Ideally, your vulnerability will encourage them to be vulnerable in return. Or it will at least motivate them to empathize with where you're coming from. Be patient with them and yourself as your friendship adjusts.

Have you ever used a pressure washer? Or seen power washing videos? I would happily power wash my entire town for free just to experience the satisfying results firsthand. If you don't know what I'm talking about, let me explain: a pressure or power washer is a super powerful hose that sprays water with enough force to blast away the gunk of an old driveway, a grubby deck, or another similar surface. The result is magnificent: with a little bit of work and patience, a surface that you didn't realize was disgusting is now shiny and clean.

Prayer, bravery, discernment, and vulnerability are the pressure washers for friendship. They are the bolt cutters to the chains that have been tying you down, the antidotes to the poison of so many relationships. Yes, they require effort and reflection, but so does anything worth doing. Friendships are worth the effort. *You* are worth the effort. You got this. You deserve wings.

4.

Bringing Jesus into Your Friendships

I love to cook.

Cooking combines two of my other great loves: eating delicious food and saving money by not frequently going out to eat.

In my quest to advance my cooking prowess, I read a lot of cookbooks. I know, this sounds very much like a grandmother activity, especially when paired with drinking tea and going to bed before 9 p.m. But I'm learning more and more that grandmother hobbies are actually the coolest, and I'm tired of pretending otherwise.

Thankfully, my friends encourage me in my cooking exploits (mostly because I share what I make with them) and often buy me cookbooks for Christmas, my birthday, or when they see one on super sale at Barnes and Noble. A couple of years ago, I received a wonderful new cookbook titled *Bavel: Modern Recipes Inspired by the Middle East*. This cookbook is gorgeous, full of pictures showcasing delicious-looking meals captured in sublime lighting. I read it cover to cover, my mouth watering like a teething baby. At the conclusion of the book, I read about the chefs who wrote the recipes and learned that the cookbook is inspired by a real-life restaurant, also called Bavel, located in Los Angeles.

Electricity crackled through my brain. This stunning restaurant that inspired this stunning cookbook is in Los Angeles. *I live* in Los Angeles (well, just outside of the city; I'm not a wealthy celebrity). I didn't have to attempt to cook this food. I could have professional chefs cook this food *for* me. I could go to this restaurant. I could go tonight! I picked up my phone and immediately called to make a reservation. Turns out there wasn't space for me that night, but I booked a table for Wednesday of the next week.

The following Wednesday, I dressed carefully and elected to wear heels (a decision I have made freely maybe four times in my entire life). I picked up a dining buddy after she got back from work, and off we zoomed to downtown Los Angeles in high spirits. I parallel parked with relative ease, and we followed Google Maps to a brick building with outdoor hanging lights and excellent shrubbery. Across the street, an unknown movie set blocked off a sidewalk to film a night shoot. This seemed like an outstanding omen.

We waltzed past the line to locate the host: "Maggie, reservation for two, 7 p.m.?"

The host flashed me a dazzling smile. "Right this way."

The host, who had to have been a model or actor taking a break from the movie set outside, gracefully led us to a nearby table.

"Enjoy your meal," he instructed us, chiseled arms gesturing us into our wicker seats.

"Oh, we will!" I declared with confidence.

And we did.

I have never had a dining experience like the one I had at Bavel that night.

First: the atmosphere. Thick hanging vines trailed down from the ceiling; white brick donned the walls; colorful tiles decorated the floor; a dimly lit bathroom flickered with candles and gold-framed mirrors; baseball-cap-wearing chefs manned fireplaces, roasting huge slabs of meat heard sizzling from your seat five feet away. Google this, please.

Second: the food. THE FOOD!

We didn't even order. Our exceptionally attractive waiter (respectfully, the entire staff was plucked off the runway) just asked us, "What are we feeling tonight?" When we replied that we were feeling hungry and adventurous, he laughed melodiously and returned with dish after dish: baba ghanoush, hummus, fried quail, soft-boiled eggs, slow roasted lamb neck shawarma, strawberry sumac and sweet cheese pastry—and finally, the simple dish that altered my brain chemistry and frequently appears in my dreams: malawach, a Yemeni flatbread made up of thin layers of pastry brushed with oil. At one point, I realized that both my friend and I had tears in our eyes. We didn't even wipe them away as we savored the best meal of entire lives.

I felt like a Kansas homebody at the base of the Eiffel Tower: out of my element and thrilled to be so. I snapped photo after photo of all the food and the hanging vines and the bar and the entryway and even the bathroom. You better believe I posted them all on social media. I downloaded the Yelp app just to leave a glowing review. I called my mom the next day and begged her to book a plane ticket to visit me so we could relive the life-changing meal. I texted every friend I knew who lived in a two-hour radius and demanded they make a reservation. I could not stop talking about Bavel.

Why?

Because I had an amazing experience. I found something incredible. I legitimately felt like a different person, and I couldn't keep it to myself. And why would I want to? When you love something, you don't keep it hidden. You share it. Especially with the people you love most.

Such is the situation we find ourselves in when it comes to God. Let's talk faith.

The author of the Letter to the Hebrews declares: "Now faith is the assurance of things hoped for, the conviction of things not seen" (Hebrews 11:1). The *Catechism of the Catholic Church* writes that "faith is both a gift of God and a human act by which the believer gives personal adherence to God who invites his response, and freely assents to the whole truth that God has revealed" (*Catechism of the Catholic Church*, Glossary). Faith is a big deal.

I don't know where you are on your faith journey.

Maybe you were raised Christian and you go to church on the weekend when your family does. Maybe you pray only occasionally when you need something. Maybe you feel really distant from a Christian identity. Or maybe, you have a strong relationship with God. Maybe prayer is part of your daily routine. Maybe you participate in a weekly Bible study, read about the lives of the saints, frequently volunteer in your local community, and feel very close to God. Wherever you're at with faith, that's an okay place to be. No matter what, there is no condemnation. But there is always room to grow.

Our faith, no matter what level, is very personal to each one of us. But it cannot be private. Faith is personal, but not private. Faith cannot be hidden. It simply cannot. This personal relationship we share with God is supposed to take over our lives! Not like a disease, but like sunshine—to illuminate and elevate every aspect of our lives. Our faith relationship cannot be a secret.

I regret to disclose that I had a secret romantic relationship when I was in high school (a bad idea on infinite levels). Well, it was partially secret. My family sort of knew about it, but I was not fully honest with them. I didn't reveal how often we met up or when or where or what we were doing (Mom, Dad, Louise: I know we have since talked about this and have moved on but once again, I apologize for my dishonesty).

At first, I thought this secret relationship was exhilarating.

It sort of felt like a *Bourne Identity* film, but without the global terrorism and threat of war. I felt sophisticated, sneaky, and generally cooler than everyone else around me. But too soon, the secrecy began to weigh on me—like a backpack stuffed with textbooks that I could never take off. I began to question my motives, and his. I couldn't remember why we were hiding. Was he ashamed of me? Was I embarrassed about him? Did he think his parents wouldn't like me? Did I think my friends wouldn't like him? Were we in love if nobody knew? You can probably predict what came next for High School Maggie. The unnecessary secrecy prompted my doomed relationship to self-implode very quickly. Love, if it is true, cannot be hidden.

God loves each one of us. Not because of what we've done or have not done or has been done to us. He loves us because of who we are, and who we are are his children. He wants to be in relationship with us. Not in an abusive or controlling relationship, but a relationship of love. This loving relationship cannot be hidden. St. Paul writes to the Romans: "For I am not ashamed of the gospel" (Romans 1:16). Paul is not ashamed of the Good News of Jesus Christ! He does not hide what God did in his life. Neither can we be ashamed of our relationship with God and try to hide it away. If we attempt to do so, it will implode.

What must we do instead?

Evangelize! We must simply share our faith and tell the world about our relationship with God! Not in an aggressive, weird, or obnoxious way. Don't shove your faith down someone's throat. Please don't do that. Rather, be genuine and kind. Honestly tell others about Jesus and what he means to you in your life.

You might say: "Maggie, I don't know much about my faith. It's pretty new to me, and there are some things about it I still don't understand." That's totally fine! You don't need a degree in theology to talk about your faith. I think it's very important to be well-formed in your faith, but that comes with time. Right now, all you need is the courage to tell other people about the amazing encounters you've had with God, and how valuable he is to you.

Just like me and Bavel! I hardly know anything about restaurants or the cooking industry or Middle Eastern cuisine or the food scene in LA. So what? I had a great time at an amazing restaurant, and that is enough qualification to tell other people about it.

You might say: "Maggie, my friends aren't religious. My parents don't attend church anymore. Most of the people at my job/school/dorm/soccer team/sorority/fraternity/theater group/etc. belong to different faith backgrounds."

Okay, then they need to hear about your relationship with God even more!

Back to Bavel (everything comes back to Bavel).

It doesn't matter if my coworkers/classmates/roommates/teammates/family once had food poisoning from Middle Eastern food. I'm certainly sorry they had a bad experience before, but this just means that they're in even *more* need of a great experience to counteract the terrible one. The people in my life might be picky eaters, or enjoy Italian food, or be vegan, or prefer takeout. Regardless, no one is disqualified from me telling them about Bavel. If they love me, they will want to hear about what I love, even if they personally don't love it (yet).

You might say: "Maggie, I don't want to act like I'm better than someone. By sharing my faith, am I being arrogant? Am I telling someone what to do? I don't want people to think that I see myself as this super righteous, holy person."

One of my favorite definitions of evangelization is this: one beggar telling another beggar where to find bread. We are all beggars. I know I am. We are burdened under the weight of chaos and dysfunction and despair, and the sin in our lives has left us spiritually starving. But miraculously, through no merit of our own, we have stumbled upon a feast. We have found free bread! We have found the bread of life—the healing and satisfaction and meaning we crave. We have found not something, but Someone. And his name is Jesus.

What kind of people would we be if we kept that information to ourselves? If you are a beggar and you don't tell other beggars about free bread, that's not a good look. If you conceal life-changing information from other beggars, from close companions, from people who have struggled and scraped by your side for years, that could be considered lazy. Selfish. Cruel. Our silence allows our friends to persist in their spiritual hunger. We must tell others! I know it's hard—trust me, I know it is. But we have to get over our fear of looking stupid and instead get to work telling people about Jesus.

You might say: "Maggie, I don't want my friendships to change. If I bring God into the relationships, that might make things weird and awkward. It will shift the whole dynamic."

I hear you. But you have nothing to worry about. God doesn't make things worse. Sure, there might be an adjustment period in your relationships once you try to make God an overt part of them. But ultimately, this is only going to bring about good stuff. Jesus sanctifies, elevates, and redeems all things, including friendships. He has come so that we might have life, and have it abundantly (John 10:10)! Jesus doesn't take away fun; he gives us ultimate joy! Maybe he will prune away bad decisions and negative habits, but in their place, he will give you lasting fulfillment and peace and freedom. Sin doesn't even come close to the true fun that comes from fearlessly living as God's child, surrounded by your brothers and sisters in Christ. Don't believe the lie that God will ruin your friendships. Boldly share your relationship with God with your friends even if you aren't positive what will happen next.

In my experience, most people don't have a relationship with God simply because they don't know how. They don't know it is actually possible, and they're unfamiliar with the concept. No one has taught them how. No one has invited them in. But that is going to change, because you are going to include the people you care about in your relationship with God. You are going to share your faith with your friends.

Here are the keys: low expectation and personal invitation.

You're going to keep your hopes in check. Your friend may not fall in love with God instantly or, honestly, ever. God alone converts hearts to himself. We trust in his timing regardless of the visible results.

And you're going to personally invite. You aren't going to abstractly wish your friend comes to Jesus; nor are you going to drop microscopic hints. You aren't going to post an Instagram story about hoping someone close to you becomes a more faithful Christian. You are going to directly, kindly, and personally invite someone.

Let me give you an analogy of what this can look like practically.

I love NBA basketball. I was raised on it, and I grew up playing basketball myself. I have been to dozens of games and watched hundreds on TV. My dad and I constantly talk about the players and coaches and statistics and MVP race. I know modern NBA basketball isn't what it once was, and the players are definitely imperfect people on and off the court. I still love the game.

My friend Marie does not. She doesn't hate sports, but she believes professional basketball is rigged. She doesn't trust the refs and the players and the coaches not to be greedy and throw the games. Honestly, she has a point, but I don't like to think about it, so I keep watching.

One time, Marie and I were at my house and decided to watch a movie. I had an NBA game playing on the TV before she arrived. But since the playoffs were really far away, I had no problem switching to another form of entertainment. As I exited away from the broadcast, Marie sighed. "I just don't understand why you like NBA."

Something clicked in my brain. The truth hit me. Maybe the reason Marie doesn't like NBA basketball is because nobody taught her about it. Maybe she's just unfamiliar with the whole thing. Maybe if she experienced it for herself, she would change her mind. Once the movie ended and Marie left, I snatched up my phone and opened the Ticketmaster app. I searched for the Los Angeles Lakers' schedule and saw a home game for this coming Friday. I texted Marie. "Hey, great to see you tonight! Want to hang out on Friday?"

"Sure," she responded. "Anything in mind?"

"I'll plan it! I'll pick you up on Friday once you're done with work."

I returned to the Ticketmaster app and, giggling with excitement, purchased two of the cheapest tickets in the arena.

On Friday, I pulled up to Marie's apartment, giddy with anticipation. As she opened the passenger door, I tossed her a yellow piece of fabric.

"What's this?" she asked, holding it up.

"It's a Lakers jersey, girl! Put it on! We're going to a Lakers game tonight! I bought us tickets!"

"Maggie." Marie frowned at me. "You know I don't like NBA basketball."

"Oh, I am well aware," I responded, lightly punching her on the shoulder. "But you like me! And I like NBA basketball. You don't have to become a super fan overnight, but we're going to the game tonight, my treat."

Marie rolled her eyes, but smiled. I shifted my GMC Terrain into drive and motored to the stadium. As we crawled along in the Los Angeles traffic, I gave Marie the lowdown on the Lakers that season. Who was on the team, who was injured, who recently got traded, who the coaches were, what the team's record was, who they were facing tonight, who I expected to win. We parked a couple blocks over from the arena and joined throngs of purple and gold-clad fans streaming toward the entrance.

"This is my friend's first Lakers game!" I announced to the crowd at large. They roared in approval. Once we got past security,

I grabbed us a couple of programs and contemplated buying a twelve-dollar hot dog. The allurement of mystery meat overpowered me, and I got us two hot dogs. We found our seats as the Lakers and their opponents, the Philadelphia 76ers, began warming up. As LeBron shot free-throws and Joel Embiid stretched, I leaned over to Marie and pointed out the players. Before tip-off, I explained the timing of the game and how many fouls the players were allowed, as well as my earnest desire to see LeBron have a chasedown block and at least one alley-oop dunk. Then the game began!

For the first half, Marie and I chatted for much of the game.

"What just happened?" she asked as the whistle blew.

"That was a charge—the offense fouled the defense. Oh okay, now there is a thirty second television time-out."

"Why are there so many time-outs?"

"Because the NBA is ultimately a business, and they rely heavily on the advertising that plays during the time-outs."

But after halftime, I stopped providing commentary and just let Marie experience the game. The drama unfolded, and I was completely sucked in. The game was close, with points exchanged each possession. I was on my feet screaming. As the fourth quarter drew to a close, Marie stood up to join me, cheering and clapping. I didn't even care that LeBron fouled out over a bogus call. I don't even remember who won that game. That wasn't the point.

The point was that as Marie and I walked to the car after the game, I asked her what she thought about her first Lakers game and if she would ever want to come to another one. "Maggie, I still don't really understand what happened, and I have a lot of questions. But I understand why you love it. Thank you for sharing it with me."

I have no idea if Marie will become a lifelong, die-hard NBA fan like me. That isn't under my control. What is under my control is introducing Marie to the NBA. Showing her why it's amazing. Answering any of her questions. Telling her about the positive impact it has had on me. Inviting her to come back.

Do you see where I'm going with this story? To be super clear, I'm making a comparison between sharing my love of NBA basketball and sharing my love of Jesus. This isn't a perfect analogy, and there's nothing morally superior about NBA basketball over college basketball or professional football. NBA basketball isn't intrinsically good, and liking or disliking it ultimately doesn't matter. But hopefully you can see the similarities: I boldly invited Marie to share in my experience, didn't judge her for her discomfort or lack of familiarity, patiently explained what was going on, and invited her to return.

We can be so hesitant to do this, to evangelize our friends. I know I have been in the past. One of my life regrets is not sharing my faith more with my middle school and high school friends. Instead of gently and personally inviting them to share in my relationship with God, I concealed it from them. Downplayed its importance in my life. Eventually, when my faith grew too large to ignore, I lashed out at them for not being on the same page. Pushed them away when our differences became too stark. Judged them for not embracing someone they never really met before. I still pray for them and ask God for forgiveness for my cowardice and selfishness all those years ago. But it literally keeps me up at night.

What I should have done was not let my fear of rejection outweigh Jesus's imperative to me and to all Christians. After Jesus rose, while ascending into heaven, he commanded those gathered around him: "Go therefore and make disciples of all nations, baptizing them in the name of the Father and of the Son and of the Holy Spirit, teaching them to observe all that I have commanded you" (Matthew 28:19). To be a Christian is to evangelize. Jesus told us to. We have to do it.

How?

Don't overcomplicate it. Don't overthink it.

Let me give you some practical examples.

Example #1: Over the weekend, your friends spend the night at your house. In the morning as you're making breakfast, you invite them to join you for a Bible study at your Church later that day. You offer to drive and then take them out for milkshakes afterwards.

Example #2: You're on a traveling basketball team that plays tournaments on the weekend. You have a three-hour break in between games and you Google a nearby church. You do the math and realize you have plenty of time to get there and back. Once you return from church and get back to the court, your teammates ask where you were. "I went to church!" you tell them. "Even when I have a lot of stuff going on, making time for my faith is really important to me."

Example #3: You're eating wings with your friends at a local restaurant and watching college football. Before you dig into your meal, you take a moment to thank God for the gift of the food in front of you and ask blessings for all those who go without. You tell your friends: "I'm going to say a quick prayer before I eat, would you like to join me?"

Example #4: You just returned from vacation and your coworkers ask about your trip. You tell them about the food you ate and the activities you did and how you went to church on Sunday. Your coworkers act surprised. You explain: "My Christian faith is really important to me, and I don't take a break from it, even on vacation. Would you like to see some pictures I took of the church and the rest of my trip?"

Example #5: You friend Carly is telling you that she's going through a tough time. You listen to her, empathize with her, and put a hand on her arm as she begins to cry. You listen patiently and don't rush her. Once she finishes unloading her heart to you, you tell her you are so sorry. You say: "When I'm struggling like you are, I like to pray. Would you mind if I pray with you right now?"

Example #6: Your church hosts a weekly speaker series. The night begins with snacks and drinks, then the talk, then a period of question and answer. You usually attend with your family, but you had the idea to invite one of your friends to join you. Connor doesn't normally go to church, but you've been spending more time together recently, and he's asked you questions about your religion. You decide it's worth a shot to invite him, even if he turns you down.

Example #7: Your aunt passed away last weekend and her funeral was held yesterday. Once you're back at work, your coworkers ask you how you're feeling. You tell them: "Obviously, this is super sad and really hard. But my aunt was a faithful woman and I truly do believe I'll see her again in heaven. I'm grateful for the gift of my faith to help me with this tough time."

Example #8: Every morning, you spend at least fifteen minutes praying with your Bible as you drink your tea before work. Your friends decided to go on a weekend camping trip, and you make sure to pack your Bible along with an extra one just in case. Early on the first morning at the campground, you sit on a folding chair around the fire and open your Bible. One of your friends unzips the tent and comes over to you.

"What are you reading?" she asks.

"The Bible. I start my morning with some tea and prayer time. Would you like to join me? I actually have another Bible with me."

Expect rejection. Expect confusion and awkward laughter. Expect bizarre and maybe even offensive comments. That's fine! That's not going to stop you from sharing the faith that is part of your life or from gently inviting them in again at another time, perhaps in another way. You can handle it. You can handle it because you're doing what God has called you to do. God never asks us to do anything alone. Jesus's final words in the Gospel of Matthew are a promise: "I am with you always, to the close of the age" (Matthew 28:20).

Jesus is with you—at every moment of your life and especially right now. He is most definitely present in your efforts to evangelize, especially in your desire to bring your friends to him, in your hopes of purifying friendships and lifting them up to God. He is with you, and he is giving you the power to share your faith. That strength comes from him alone, but we cooperate with him. You can do it.

5.

How to End a Friendship

I started dating a lacrosse player when I was sixteen years old. I thought the relationship was perfect—it was not. It ended in spectacular fashion, at prom no less, and I felt like it happened right out of a movie, but not in a good way. The breakup started on the dance floor and finished with me lying on my bedroom floor, crying so hard I almost threw up into my pile of unfolded (but clean) laundry. I suffered through weeks of tears and pints of ice cream, not leaving the couch and taking minimal showers. It was awful.

But that was nothing, *nothing*, compared to the heartbreak I endured when some of my female friendships fell apart. I have had the misfortune of going through several friendship fallouts, and there is no pain like it. I think most of us understand that romantic partners will come and go. But not our friends. We expect our friends to be in our lives forever. I certainly did. When I was younger, I dreamed of being a bridesmaid at my friends' weddings, buying a house near them so we could raise our kids together, and moving into the same senior living center to finish out our golden years. Not many of us foresee our platonic friendships having an end date.

Growing up, my family would often embark on cross-country road trips over the holidays to visit our cousins and aunts and uncles around the United States. My parents refused to buy a DVD player for our minivan, so my sister and I devised our own entertainment. We whiled away the hours playing I-spy or the alphabet game, trying to spot license plates from all fifty states ("How it is even possible to find Hawaii? There is an actual ocean separating Hawaii from the rest of the United States!") and the billboard that made us laugh the hardest. Often, I rested my head on the car door and gazed out the window, passively observing the vehicles motoring next to us. I noticed that some cars would drive alongside our van for hours of the trip. It felt like a few of them rode next to us the entire time. But what was more common was for a car to drive nearby for a few miles and then exit off. Or change lanes. Or fall behind. Or speed on ahead. Some cars stuck around, most did not. That is part of driving.

That is also part of friendship. Some friends stick around for the whole ride. It's wonderful when that happens, but it very rarely does. We might want the same exact people around us for our entire lives, but that doesn't always occur. Nor should it. Most friendships are around for a few years before they exit off. Or before you exit off. Is this hard? Absolutely. But it doesn't have to be bad. It could actually be one of the best and healthiest things for you, though it needs to happen in the right way.

What are the wrong ways for a friendship to end? I will give you two ways that I have personally experienced, and that I definitely don't recommend pursuing.

Unhealthy Friendship Ending #1: A blowup.

Unhealthy Friendship Ending #1 is not pretty. It is not mature. It involves a lot of shouting and a lot of accusations. It is meant to humiliate. Typically, it happens in a public place to ensure maximum drama. You see this a lot on reality television, but **Unhealthy Friendship Ending #1** also happens in real life. It happened to me. Toward the end of high school, one of my friends realized I was serious about my Christian faith. And even though it was personally challenging for me at times, I still submitted to the authority of Jesus and believed in all of the Church's teachings. Jessica, my soon-to-be-ex-friend, did not like this. Two weeks before graduation, she accosted me outside of the dining hall. She screamed at me and called me a hateful person for everyone around us to hear. She got right up in my face and shoved me, and I thought she was going to lean back and punch me in the jaw. Honestly, she might have, if some of my other friends didn't pull me away and help me leave the scene immediately.

Unhealthy Friendship Ending #1 can happen in person, like what happened to me and Jessica. But what's becoming more popular is a subtler form of **Unhealthy Friendship Ending #1**, through social media and the internet. Spamming someone's profile with cruel comments. Making a video exposing a former friend. Sending anonymous messages to someone's account. Leaving a dozen malicious voicemails. While I could physically remove myself from Jessica, it's not easy to remove yourself from online attacks. Your phone is with you almost everywhere you go. Therefore, this is an especially cowardly and nefarious thing to do. Whether you're attacked online or you attack somebody else, it's unacceptable. Even if there are legitimate reasons to end the friendship, this tactic cannot be tolerated. Friendships are allowed to end, but bullying is never allowed.

Unhealthy Friendship Ending #2: Ghosting.

When I was little, my favorite Halloween costume was a ghost. I think I repeated this costume at least five years in a row. With just a few bed sheets, I perfected the look. I loved being a ghost then, but I refuse to be a ghost now. "Ghosting" is a modern term referring to when someone deliberately cuts another person out of their life without any warning. No explanation. A relationship is completely dropped out of the blue. The sudden severing of communication is compared to death, as if someone died and then became a ghost. I regret to report that this practice is horrifically common in romantic situations, but sadly, also within friendships.

Here is a made-up example of how **Unhealthy Friendship Ending #2** can play out:

You and your high school best friend Jaime carpool together every morning. You don't share any of the same classes, but you meet up in the hallways and eat lunch together at your usual table. You're both on the varsity soccer team and hang out with the athletic trainers before practice. If you have an away game, you sit next to each other on the bus and share headphones, listening to music to get yourselves ready to compete. Before the game, you run drills together. After the game, you swing by your favorite fast food joint to split some fries and analyze both of your performances. After you go back to your respective homes, you often FaceTime as you do your homework or text each other on and off throughout the rest of the evening.

One day, you pull up to Jaime's house to drive her to school as usual. She's not sitting on her deck waiting for you like she normally does. You text her that you're here. She doesn't text you back. You wait a few minutes before walking up her driveway and knocking on her front door. Jaime's younger brother pops his head outside. "Hey, Andrew, is Jaime ready to go?" Andrew tells you that Jaime already left for school. "Oh. Are you sure?"

"I'm positive," Andrew tells you before turning away. "She's gone." You feel confused, but you get back in your car to drive to school. You'll ask Jaime about it once you see her soon. But you don't see her. She isn't waiting for you by the vending machines in between classes.

At lunch time, she isn't sitting with any of your other friends at your standard table. "Have you seen Jaime today?" you ask your classmates.

"Yeah, I've seen her around, but I haven't talked to her yet," one of them tells you.

You're definitely beginning to feel weird. You text Jaime again after lunch, but still receive no response. After school, you get your ankles taped by your athletic trainer before your game. Jaime is not in the training room. Something feels off. You finally see her in the parking lot with the rest of your soccer teammates, waiting for the bus. You go up to her to ask her what's up, but she boards the bus before you get the chance. By the time you get on the bus, Jaime is already sitting with one of the other forwards. You sit near her, but she avoids eye contact with you. You don't have a clue what is going on.

Jaime does not warm up with you, but instead stretches with the other players on offense. You stretch with your defensive teammates. The game passes in a daze. After the final whistle, Jaime still doesn't talk to you, and she rides on the bus back with a different teammate. Once the bus arrives back at school, she gets in her car by herself to drive away. All without looking at you once. You drive to McDonalds, as is your and Jaime's tradition, but you pick up fries for only yourself. You snap a picture of your food and send it to Jaime, but you know she won't respond. And she doesn't. The next day repeats itself almost exactly the same way. You see Jaime around, but she never sits with you at lunch or on the bus anymore. And you never FaceTime as you do your math homework or get fries together after a game again. You have no idea what happened. Jaime never tells you.

Unhealthy Friendship Ending #1 Lays It All Out There. Nothing is left unsaid at a blowup. The opposite is true with Unhealthy Friendship Ending #2. Everything is left unsaid when you're ghosted! Being ignored like this, without explanation, numbs your brain. When I have gone through this, I felt like I was a victim of a sadistic form of torture at the hands of masked operatives. I so badly wanted to climb up a nearby water tower and scream at the top of my lungs: "What happened?! What did I do wrong?? How can you do this to me!?" Again, even if there are truly valid reasons for ending a friendship, ghosting is never the way to do it.

Here's what I suggest instead:

Healthy Friendship Ending #1: Direct Communication.

Healthy Friendship Ending #2: Slowly Stepping Back.

Both require real maturity. I have learned that maturity doesn't necessarily come with age. Ideally, it should, but unfortunately that's not always the case. I define maturity as the ability to be honest and to receive honesty. When you're mature, you're confident of your feelings. Because of that, you can express them without fear. You don't play games. You don't gossip. You don't lie or withhold information. You don't downplay your perspective. Instead, you communicate the truth as kindly as you can, even if you know that someone might struggle to hear it. Even if it's hard for you to say it out loud.

There are two sides to my definition of maturity. You must also be open to hearing the truth from someone else—even if it paints you in an unflattering or unfair light. You must have the strength to humbly accept what can feel harsh. As calmly as you can, you receive someone else's feelings. Can you cry about this later? Of course you can! Let yourself process in any way you need to, as long as you don't play games either. You don't gossip either. You don't lie or withhold information either. You don't drag in other people who have no part. You can of course ask your parents or a trusted adult for guidance, but you don't involve your peers.

Maturity is a key part of **Healthy Friendship Ending #1** and **Healthy Friendship Ending #2**. Here is what else you need. In chapter 3, I strongly recommended prayer, bravery, discernment, and vulnerability when assessing a friendship. Voicing some of your concerns is a necessary practice that needs to be implemented *throughout* the relationship, not just at its conclusion. Both of these endings are a continuation of what should have already been occurring. I think it's unfair to deny someone a chance to change or rectify some of their poor behavior. A few chapters back, I included this example of vulnerability on page 42:

> Matt, I was bullied a lot when I was younger. It was awful and I never want to go through that again. I don't want to be bullied in my friendships. I don't think you do it on purpose, but sometimes I feel like the butt of a joke to you, and I really don't like feeling that way. I want to laugh and have fun with you, but I don't want you to make fun of me. Can you help me with this?

Say you have this conversation with Matt. And you do it in person. If for some reason that is just not possible, you do it over a phone call or on FaceTime. You never do it via text or Snapchat. You talk to Matt face-to-face, and he takes it to heart. Matt hears you out, says he never meant to act that way, and maybe he even apologizes. He makes a change, starts behaving differently, and you stop feeling belittled by him. You don't feel like the punch line of a joke anymore. Rather, you feel like Matt includes you in on the jokes instead of making them at your expense. Over the next few months, you see a difference and you feel different in your friendship. You feel supported. You feel more confident. You trust Matt again. Your friendship isn't perfect, but it's overcoming this obstacle and is stronger than ever.

That is the ideal situation. But what if that doesn't happen? What if Matt shrugs off your disclosure? He might say: "That's crazy!" after you tell him your feelings. "That's not what's happening. That's just my sense of humor, how I always act. You're being too sensitive." As the months go on, you feel worse and worse about the friendship. You now dread going to events with Matt because you're certain he's going to make fun of you at some point. After hanging out with him, you don't feel energized and happy like you used to. When you're with him now, you feel small and hesitant. You're nervous that every time he laughs, it's going to be at your expense. You don't want to be around Matt anymore.

You have spent significant time praying about this, being brave, discerning, and practicing vulnerability. And you know something has to change.

You have two choices.

Healthy Friendship Ending #1: Direct Communication.

This is going to be a hard conversation. But you can do hard things. **Healthy Friendship Ending #1** looks like a straightforward discussion about why you don't want to be part of this friendship anymore. It's clear, yet charitable. It's unapologetic, but sympathetic. It involves just you and the friend. It cannot be done in a group setting and no unrelated people can be involved. It's not an unjust accusation, but an honest explanation of everything that you're feeling.

Here is an example of what it might look like: You and Matt finish up a workout together at the gym. You walk back to your separate cars in the parking lot. Before Matt gets into his car, you say: "Hey, Matt, do you have a second? I want to talk to you about something." If he agrees, you take a deep breath and try your best to keep your voice steady. "Matt, you have been one of my best friends for years. But I'm having a really hard time still being friends with you right now. A couple of months ago I brought this up to you; I told you that I felt you were making fun of me. That was hard for me to admit to you, and you just brushed me off. And you continued acting the same way, laughing with our friends about everything I do and making me feel stupid and childish all the time. I mean it—you are one of my best friends. But I don't want to be around you anymore when you keep making me feel this way."

How will Matt respond? That is not up to you. What is up to you is saying what you need to say. Matt might yell at you. He might shrug his shoulders. He might laugh at you and accuse you of being a baby. He might tell your other friends that you were a jerk to him. If that's the case, then Matt is making your decision easier. You deserve a friend who respects you more than that. **Healthy Friendship Ending #1** is difficult. But it's a relief to get it off your chest.

Here is another option.

Healthy Friendship Ending #2: Slowly Stepping Back.

Healthy Friendship Ending #2 isn't nearly as heartless as ghosting. It's not ignoring someone, blocking them, or cutting them out entirely. But it does involve limiting communication. Less texting. Less time spent together. Not initiating get-togethers. You aren't the first to reach out. You can still talk to and see your friend, but you exert significantly less effort into the friendship. You're not doing this to be mean. You're doing this to protect yourself.

As a refresher, here is another example of vulnerability from page 47:

> Hannah, I miss spending quality time with you. Ever since you started dating your new boyfriend, I've felt left out. I've had friends choose their boyfriends over me in the past, and it makes me feel

> replaceable. I know you don't mean to make me feel this way, but it makes me feel like you don't really care about me anymore. Can you help me with this?

You might have this conversation with Hannah as you eat grilled cheese sandwiches at your favorite café. And Hannah might really listen. She might let you say everything you need to say and ask for more clarification, nodding as you tell her more. Then she may apologize. She may tell you that she cares for you and values your friendship. This is her first romantic relationship, and she's still figuring out what that looks like in her life. She promises to make sure you feel included. And she follows through on that promise. Even though Hannah keeps dating her boyfriend, you no longer feel like a second-best option. She reaches out to you and schedules hang outs. You spend time together, just the two of you. You start to relax. You feel more confident in the friendship as Hannah continues to prove to you that you're a valuable part of her life. The risk to be vulnerable paid off.

That is the ideal situation. But what if that doesn't happen? What if you pour your heart out to Hannah over grilled cheese sandwiches, and she rolls her eyes? She could say: "Maggie, calm down. I'm in a serious romantic relationship and of course I'm going to be spending more time with Joshua than with you! Why aren't you more supportive? I guess you're just jealous you don't have a boyfriend." As the weeks unfold, Hannah spends more and more time with Joshua. She sits with him and his friends at lunch and goes on dates with him every weekend. When she does hang out with you, she's distracted and texting Joshua the whole time. You get the feeling she's only spending time with you because he's busy with homework or band practice. Now just the thought of Hannah makes you feel hot with anger. You don't want to be a consolation prize anymore. You want to be done.

You have spent significant time praying about this, being brave, discerning, and practicing vulnerability. And you know something has to change. You might decide not to initiate **Healthy Friendship Ending #1** of Direct Communication with Hannah. Maybe you were so hurt by Hannah blatantly disregarding the feelings you shared at the café that you decide it's not worth it to be vulnerable again. That's completely understandable and a reasonable choice. **Healthy Friendship Ending #2** of Slowly Stepping Back doesn't involve confrontation, which may appear easier. But it also doesn't provide you the chance to explain why you're making the conscious choice that you are. If you can accept that, here is what **Healthy Friendship Ending #2** of Slowly Stepping Back can look like.

You don't text Hannah when you hear a song by a band that both of you like. You don't ask her to get Mexican food with you next Friday. You don't wait for her after class. You don't seek her out in the lunchroom or in the hallways. You don't ask to study together in the library before your test on Thursday. When you see her around school as you inevitably will, you make eye contact and smile. But you might not stop to talk. Or if you do, you only chat for a few seconds before you move on. If she texts you, you respond back. But you don't ask a follow-up question. You wait for Hannah to reach out first, for her to be the one to ask you to spend time together, for her to display any interest in the continuation of your friendship. But you're unsurprised when she does not. Because Hannah has shown you who she is, and when people do that, you believe them. Hannah is not your enemy. You still love her and care for her and pray for her. But you do this from afar. You and Hannah were on the same highway next to each other for a while, but now you are signaling with your blinker and exiting off. It can be so painful, but you have to let the fade happen.

Healthy Friendship Ending #1 and **Healthy Friendship Ending #2** might seem callus. Harsh. Nasty. But they're not. Too often we give up so much for people who would never consider sacrificing for us. Both these approaches are about establishing boundaries. Boundaries are a sign something is worth protecting. That something is you—YOU are worth protecting. The prophet Isaiah tells us that we are precious in the eyes of God, that God honors us and loves us (Isaiah 43:4). God treats us that way. And so should everyone else, especially our closest friends.

Healthy Friendship Ending #1 and **Healthy Friendship Ending #2** are both open for reconciliation. Jesus is always open to reconcile with us, and we look to him as a model for all things. While still protecting ourselves, we should remain open to restoring the friendship. But only if there is evidence of visible and tangible change. I discourage resuming the friendship just because you feel lonely or sentimental or because you bump into each other in a small, independent bookstore on the coast of Maine over the Christmas holidays when you both live in Texas, and this coincidence feels destined. Change must occur. Old habits must be broken. There must be a clear path of moving forward. Otherwise, we will fall back into the same harmful patterns, and the friendship will resume its negative effect on you.

But I believe people can change. God knows his children can change. Through the grace of God, change is always possible, even if it happens on a different timeline than we would like. A friend could realize what they've done wrong and put in effort to improve the friendship that they destroyed. Your cars can merge back onto the same highway and drive next to each other again. If that happens, hallelujah! But we cannot wait around for it. Regardless, you are valuable and worthy, and the people around you must recognize that. Friends cannot be sources of insecurity and anxiety. They are designed to be sources of love and peace and joy and comfort. And if they are not, you must have the courage to do something about it.

6.

Making New Friends

Last chapter was a tough one. Removing yourself from toxic friendships is definitely challenging. It is so hard. But trust me, it's worth it in the long run. One of the many benefits is that it opens you up to new friendships. You cannot receive something new if your hand is closed around something else. You have made the difficult but right decision to open up your hands—and God is going to give you something new! Can this be intimidating? Absolutely. But it can also be very exciting.

When you're on the lookout for new friends, here's something you need to know: everyone wants new friends. Okay, rarely you might find someone who claims they don't want to hang out with anyone new. I mean this as kindly as possible, but anyone who says that typically isn't the kind of person you want to be close friends with anyway. Even if they have a really busy work schedule and a well-established friend group, all the best people I know are open to welcoming new people into their friendship circles. You are not alone in your desire for companionship! It's not weird or embarrassing to want new friends. Don't be ashamed.

I think the best way to develop new friendships can happen in two ways:

New Friendships Option #1: Elevating the friendships we already have.

New Friendships Option #2: Initiating entirely new friendships.

Let's start with the first one.

New Friendships Option #1: Elevating the friendships we already have.

These are the people you sit with at lunchtime. The fellow lifeguard with whom you have been working for the past year, your co-captain on the soccer team, the people in your study group, the classmate that you have been assigned to work with on a monthlong project, the people in your church youth group, the other parents at the tee ball league, the person who spots you when you lift weights. You know their names and a little bit about them. But you might not consider them friends because the relationship is so basic. Maybe your bond only exists out of necessity or convenience. That's fine! That's a great place to start.

My junior year of college, I enrolled in five classes. Three on Monday, Wednesday, and Friday and two on Tuesday and Thursday. At the end of the first week of the semester, I lifted my backpack onto my shoulders and was walking out of my final class when I felt someone tap me on the shoulder. I turned around and saw a tall girl who looked vaguely familiar.

"Hey, Maggie!" she said.

"Yeah?" I asked, confused and feeling slightly nervous. "Who are you?"

She smiled in a bemused sort of way. "You really don't recognize me?"

I blinked.

"My name is Rebecca. We have five classes together. Literally all of our classes are together every single day of the week. I think we should be friends."

"Oh!" I said. "Okay! Want to get lunch right now?"

Five years later, I wore a pale blue chiffon dress and stood up on the altar next to Rebecca as she and her husband entered into the sacrament of marriage. Rebecca is one of my best friends to this day. We started as students from different parts of the country, living in different dorms, in different grades, with different friend groups, hobbies, and senses of humor. And we ended up dear friends. Every meaningful friendship starts somewhere.

Here are a couple suggestions on how to initiate **New Friendships Option #1**. Test the waters and see if you can take the friendships to the next level. When you're sitting in class and chatting with the people around you waiting for the teacher to arrive, mention that your grandma is sick (obviously, if your grandma isn't sick, please don't lie). Or share that you're not sure what you're going to do over the summer. Or that you're hesitant about trying out for the musical. Or that you're relieved your dad got a new job. Or something similar. Something personal. If you're in math class, see if you can talk about things unrelated to math. If you're at the gym, initiate a conversation about something other than fitness. If you're at band practice, try to talk about a topic that doesn't concern music.

See if you can steer the conversation past what is right in front of you into more significant waters. If the people around you react in kind, great! Keep that energy going. If they're neutral, that's also fine! Keep trying! Unfortunately, there's a chance they might make a weird face and belittle your disclosure. If that happens, you have nothing to worry about. They're the ones who are immature and made it awkward. You can try again another time in another way, or decide that it's best to spend time working on other friendships.

You want to try to talk about something meaningful, and you also want to start asking thought-provoking questions. The questions can be totally random like, "Would you rather never have to sleep again or never have to breathe again?" or "What is your favorite form of potato?" Questions like these can launch the conversation into wild and hilarious places you never would have visited otherwise. I keep a few zany ice-breaker questions in my mental back pocket so I can whip them out if conversation ever begins to run dry. They always prove to lighten the mood and spice up what might be initially bland. [Please see the appendix for a long list of my favorite conversation starters.]

Or, you can ask more standard questions related to the context in which you know someone. Like: "What are you looking forward to after graduation?" or "Why did you decide to learn the piano?" or "What is your favorite part about running?" or "I know what your major is, but what job did you want to do when you were little?" or "Who or what inspired you to become an artist?" or "If you never had to go to work again, what would you want to do with your life?" Open the door. Give someone space to share. More often than not, people feel flattered when someone asks them an interesting or personal question. That so rarely happens anymore. Our conversations are usually so transactional or self-centered. But we can change that. Human beings like talking about things that they are passionate about. I know I do! Take the time to figure out what that is for someone else. [See the appendix for some ideas!]

Asking thoughtful questions and listening intently for the response also takes the pressure off you in the conversation. You don't have to become a stand-up comedian or the most interesting person in the world! You can just be you, with ears open. You're not in the conversation for the express purpose of receiving laughter and admiration. You're just trying to see someone for who they are: valuable, unique, and worth getting to know. That is why careful listening and posing intentional questions is essential whether you desire to be friends with someone or not. People in general are worth the time and effort to get to know, even the most shy and excluded and socially awkward ones. And they just might surprise you.

Here is another recommendation on how to take basic friendships to the next level. After beginning to discuss more substantial topics, initiate a hangout outside of the original context where you met. I remember going out for ice cream with a few of my classmates after an exam for which we all studied together for weeks. Walking home with a teammate after a softball game not just because we both lived nearby but because we were talking about our favorite book series. Attending a concert with a coworker after we realized we both really like the same band. Learning that the person next to me at pottery class also loves Japanese food and getting sushi together after our final class. Going to a cocktail bar with a new friend from Bible study after learning she just moved to town and is eager to explore the area.

When you remove the friendship out of its familiar environment, a change begins to happen. Instead of just being "work friends" or "friends from school" or "the girl who lives down the hall from me" or "my friend from the rock-climbing gym," the label shifts. They begin to just become "friends" without further explanation.

You might say: "Maggie, that's all fine. But you don't get it. I have zero friends. I truly have no one around me. I can't elevate friendships when I literally don't have any. I'm completely alone." I understand it might feel that way. Sometimes, I open my closet and declare, "I have nothing to wear!" even though clothes are spilling out of my closet and trying to escape down the stairs. I might feel like I don't have anything to wear, but I also might change my mind if I start rummaging around in the back and trying some different combinations. Same thing with friendships. If you're trying to survive the zombie apocalypse by isolating yourself in a remote village in the deep north with only your faithful dog for company, well, I guess you're exempt. You really do have no one else. But if that is *not* your current situation, you absolutely have people around you who could become your friends. All we need to do is rummage around in the back and try some different combinations.

New Friendships Option #2: Initiating entirely new friendships.

Take a second and think about this. I encourage you to jot this down on a piece of paper or on a note in your phone. Specifically identify some people you don't know that well but are already loosely in your orbit. That might be a student in your history class, someone on your basketball team, an employee who clocks in at the same time as you, fellow performers in your theater group, someone in your book club, other gym rats who work out at the same time as you, someone in your chess club, a fellow caffeine addict who is always at the same coffee shop as you, another young mom at the same pick-up line waiting to collect her kids from school, another runner who frequents the same trail as you, and so on. If you're a preteen or a teenager, you want to keep your eyes open for people who are around your same age. If you're a young adult or an adult, the age difference begins to fade away and doesn't matter as much. These people are your potential new friends. You just need to give the ball a nudge to get it rolling down the friendship hill.

Here's the plan:

Step 1: Think of people you either vaguely interact with or just exist in the same space on a regular basis. Bonus points if you can think of people who share the same hobbies or values as you (such as people you meet at church or while volunteering).

Step 2: Smile and introduce yourself.

Step 3: Ask a question.

Step 4: Repeat Steps 2–3 the next time you see them.

Here are some examples:

Example #1: Every Saturday, you like to sketch at your favorite coffee shop. You often see someone else sitting nearby also drawing in an open notebook. One Saturday, you recognize that same person waiting in line in front of you to order. You say "Hey, my name is Maggie. I see you in here a lot. What are you working on?" Next week if you see her again, you say: "Hi, Cassie! My name is Maggie. We met here last week. What are you planning on sketching today?"

Example #2: At your Thursday Bible study, you notice a new attendee. You sit next to him and introduce yourself. "Hi! I haven't seen you here before. I'm so glad you're here! Do you live nearby?" Next Thursday, you chat with Brian again as you help yourself to snacks. "Hi, Brian! We met here last time. How has your week been so far?"

Example #3: You're working on improving your jump shot before the basketball season and spend at least an hour a day in the gym. For the last few weeks, you've seen another basketball player working on her foul shots at a nearby hoop. When your ball bounces toward her side of the court, you jog over and say: "Hey, my name is Maggie. I've seen you practicing in here a lot. What team do you play for?" Tomorrow when you're back at the gym and you see Paige, you wave at her. "Hi, Paige, it's Maggie from yesterday. How are you feeling about tryouts coming up?"

Example #4: At Spanish tutoring, you see a student you recognize but know is in the grade above you. As both of you exit the school and walk to the parking lot, you say hi and introduce yourself. "I've seen you around, but I don't know your name. What Spanish class are you in?" At the next tutoring session, reintroduce yourself and ask about how he's been handling the homework.

Example #5: Your driver's ed class attracts students from all over your town who go to different schools. You typically sit near the same person. When you arrive to your fourth class, you sit down next to that person and say: "Hey, my name is Maggie. I recognize you from our last couple classes. What school do you go to?" At your next driver's ed say, "Hi, Sadie! My name is Maggie–I met you last week. Have you had a chance to get in more practice hours?"

Example #6: You're lacing up your shoes at the start of your favorite trail when you see a familiar runner stretching nearby. Before you start your run, you wave and introduce yourself: "Hi! I've seen you here before. Are you training for an upcoming race?" Keep your eyes open for Brandon the next time you're at the trail. If you see him again, remind him of your name and ask him how his training is going.

Example #7: After rehearsal, approach one of the performers who is also in the chorus. Say something like: "Hi, my name is Maggie. This is my first time with this production company. Have you acted here before?" At your next rehearsal, say hello and remind them of your name. "Hi, Clare. It's Maggie. I'm in the chorus with you. How has it been memorizing your song lyrics?"

Example #8: You park your car at the local preschool and walk over to the flagpole, where your son will meet you once he gets out of school. You recognize another young mom standing nearby. You make eye contact and say, "Hi, I've seen you here before. My name is Maggie. How old is your kid?" Tomorrow when you're back at the pickup line and see Elaine again, you reintroduce yourself. "Hi, Elaine! My name is Maggie. I finally said hi to you for the first time yesterday. How has your day been going so far?"

For New Friendships Option #2, you want to try your best to remember someone's name once they tell it to you. That way when you see them again, you can follow up and call them by their name. This communicates to the other person: "You are memorable to me. You stick out to me." And, by extension: "I value you." People claim they're bad at remembering names. I get it, names can be challenging, but a lot of times, I think people take the easy route and have not actually tried to remember. Here is my trick to remember names. Once someone tells you their name, repeat their name out loud and try to use it multiple times in conversation.

From Example #3 at the gym: "Your name is Paige? P-A-I-G-E? Cool, my cousin is also named Paige. It's nice to meet you, Paige. If you want, Paige, I can grab your rebounds for a few shots because I need a break to catch my breath." You might think it sounds kind of silly, but in reality, it doesn't. People often like hearing their name said out loud. And the repetition forces your brain to remember. Once the interaction has ended, write their name down on a piece of paper or in your phone with a short description: "Paige, gym, sophomore at Eastbrook High School." Then, the next time you cross paths, you call them by their name and build off your previous conversation: "Hey, Paige. Good to see you again! My name is Maggie—I was shooting hoops here yesterday. Did you watch the NBA playoffs last night?"

You might say: "Maggie, this is nuts. This seems so calculated and forced. I feel creepy planning this out." I hear you, but this isn't being creepy. Being creepy is following someone out of the coffee shop or from the gym to their home and hiding in a tree all night, watching them with binoculars. If you do that, I recommend you turn yourself over to the authorities.

We have to get rid of this false idea that friendships are supposed to happen "naturally" or "randomly." Maybe that happened when you were three years old and you became friends with the person next to you in the sandbox because you happened to live near the same park. But when you mature past the age of a toddler, you can't sit around at home and expect someone to break down your door and force you to become their new best friend. Having a friendship plan isn't weird. It makes it organized and intentional.

When we care about something, we make it organized and intentional. You want to pray more? You make a plan to read ten verses from the New Testament every morning as you eat your oatmeal. You want to exercise more? You make a plan to attend a weight lifting class four times a week. You want to read more? You make a plan to read at least half a chapter of a book before bed. You want to improve your grades? You make a plan to study in the library every day immediately after class. You want to get a new job? You make a plan to submit three resumes per day. You want to improve your finances? You make a plan to cut down on eating out and clothing purchases. Making something organized and intentional signals to your body and mind that it's important, and you're going to prove it by your actions. Why should friendship be the exception? It shouldn't. It's not.

Elevating current friendships and finding brand new friends both require what I like to call **Essential Friendship Tool #1** and **Essential Friendship Tool #2.**

Essential Friendship Tool #1: Talking.

We have to talk. Talking seems basic and almost not worth mentioning, but it's pivotal. It's got to happen. There's nothing wrong with being more on the quiet side. That's totally fine! But in friendships, especially at the beginning, when we're just getting to know someone, we have to push ourselves past what might feel naturally comfortable. What feels naturally comfortable for me is lying in my bed all day watching YouTube videos and eating brownies. Unfortunately, I can't do that every day. If I want to have a full, meaningful life, I have to push myself past what feels naturally comfortable and make things happen! That is what you have to do in relationships.

We have to talk with our friends, new and old. We must engage in and contribute to the conversation. Otherwise, we're detracting from it. One time after I graduated college, I was sitting in the dugout of my local kickball league chatting with some of my teammates. We were joined by some players on another team who we played against last week. We became a big group, sitting around for over an hour, chatting and munching on sunflower seeds. That was the first time I met Dana. As the months went on, I hung out with Dana multiple times at the kickball park and at nearby restaurants after the games. And I never once heard her speak. Not a single word. I honestly thought maybe she had a speech impediment or was deaf or hard of hearing. But I learned that wasn't the case—she had no physical speech limitations. She just didn't talk. I'm sure Dana is a wonderful person, but I'll never know. I didn't learn much about her at all because her mouth never opened.

Maybe you've always been shy. Maybe groups intimidate you. Maybe you're nervous that you'll say the wrong thing, so you would rather not say anything at all. I get that! I'm not saying to change your personality. I'm saying that we have to make the effort. We have to talk. Otherwise, we become unintentional black holes. Our persistent silence sucks the energy out of what's going on around us. When we sit back and refuse to speak in group settings, we expect everyone else to do the social labor. We cannot give the people around us the silent treatment.

Once in my wild and reckless youth, I tried out the silent treatment. As a teenager, I got into a fight with my parents (not a rare occurrence for me at the time). I wanted to do something entirely unreasonable and my parents calmly, yet firmly, told me no. I was furious. But I didn't take out my anger by screaming, slamming my door, or sneaking out. I tried something new: the silent treatment. And I'm naturally a yapper; I really enjoy talking. So this was a brand new tactic that I maliciously employed against my parents. I didn't talk to them; I didn't even look at them for six whole days. Six days! My family has been through a lot of hardship: death and illness and unemployment, among other things. But my family still says that the most challenging time in our history was that six-day period. Did my silent treatment succeed in getting me what I wanted? Of course not! It succeeded in tearing my family's relationship apart. We have since reconciled and moved on, but my silent treatment caused a lot of damage.

There's this idea floating around that the opposite of love is hate. I disagree. I think the opposite of love is indifference—a total lack of concern. At least hatred is an acknowledgement of the other. Indifference doesn't even bother. I know this isn't what so many people mean to do, but their silence often comes across as indifference. Indifference isn't how you attract friends. Indifference is how you push them away, how you tear the relationship apart. We need to talk.

What do we talk about? Anything! Everything! We can talk about "shallow" things. I remember one time sitting in a smoothie shop with my friend from middle school when she said to me: "There's nothing wrong with being shallow. You won't drown." I was so impressed by that statement that I took a can of black paint I found in the basement and painted it out on my bedroom door. I still think that sentiment is profound. We don't need to be philosophers all the time! We can talk about the reoccurring dreams we have, our favorite Taylor Swift songs, the movie we can't wait to see in theaters, our ideal sandwich, the silliest things we'd buy if we won $50 million, or just what happened in our day. Those are great topics of conversation.

But we also cannot be afraid to go deep. To talk about the real stuff: our hopes and dreams and fears and aspirations and insecurities. You know the kind of conversations that can happen at three in the morning at a sleepover, or on a long road trip? When everything is dark so you can't really see anyone's faces and you're so tired that your walls are down? I remember spending the night at a friend's house once and climbing outside her bedroom window to sit with her on the roof. As the sun began to slip beneath the clouds, she turned to me and out of the blue declared, "I don't actually know if I believe in love." Okay, amazing! Let's get deep! Those conversations are where it's at. Emotional vulnerability leads to emotional closeness, and our friendship definitely grew after that conversation on the roof.

I've had people say to me, "Maggie, when I'm with people, I never know what to say. My mind goes blank, and I just can't think of anything." Don't worry. Spending time with friends is not a competition for who can come up with the wittiest remark or the most adventurous anecdote. The best way to contribute to a conversation is to listen.

This leads me to the next tool.

Essential Friendship Tool #2: Listening.

Listening is entirely underrated. Too often we're not paying attention to what people are actually saying. Instead, we're focusing on drafting our next comment. Conversation is a dialogue, not multiple monologues. We're not exchanging impressive independent statements, we're building off each other. Building off each other happens best by listening.

The Christmas I turned twenty years old, I met up with my friend Kim, who I had not seen in a while. We enrolled in different colleges, and over the break, we decided to catch up at our favorite bakery downtown. Nibbling on scones and sipping our lattes by the fireplace, I nodded as Kim told me all about the past couple months of her life. She talked about her classes and teachers and friends and roommate and crushes and what she did on the weekends and her plans for next semester. And I was so happy to hear it! But my latte grew cold as she told me story after story without asking anything about me. Finally, Kim took a deep breath and leaned toward me across the table. "Okay, your turn. Tell me all about how you're doing."

"Oh, okay!" I responded. "Well, probably my favorite part about this past year has been my—" I didn't even finish my sentence before I noticed Kim's eyes darting down toward the phone she clutched in her lap. Her fingers began to move atop the phone. Her thumbs weren't punching the screen in unison, meaning she wasn't texting someone. Instead, her thumb was continually sliding up, which meant she was scrolling. She was looking at a social media feed instead of listening to me, who she hadn't seen in four months. I felt my heart drop out of my chest.

Not being listened to causes unique and sharp pain. Isn't it the worst when you feel like your teacher isn't listening to you when you try to ask a question? Isn't it the worst when it seems like your parents aren't listening to you when you tell them about football practice? Isn't it the worst when your friend chooses to focus on social media instead of the real-life social interaction they're currently having with you? It's truly the worst when you're ignored. It makes you feel uninteresting and unnecessary. You feel like the other person is uninvested in continuing the friendship.

I'm going to go on a rant for a second. We *have* to put our phones away. It has gotten completely out of hand. Use your phones when you're alone and bored or waiting to board your plane at the airport. That's fine. But when we're interacting with other people, the phones have to be out of sight. It's way too common for people to be with others while using their phones to text or casually browse the internet or scroll social media or play games. Since it happens all the time, we've become desensitized to how rude this behavior actually is.

When we do this, when we're actively using our phones instead of giving our full attention to the people around us, we're communicating a clear message. Whether we intend to or not, we're saying: My phone is more important than you are. You don't matter to me as much as the device in my hand. I choose playing Minecraft over listening to you. I would rather watch a video about a Caesar salad wrap from a Brooklyn bodega than pay attention to you. I prefer to text someone two hundred miles away from me instead of opening my mouth and talking to you, the person standing a foot away from me.

I like my phone. I use it all the time! I have friends all over the world with whom I wouldn't be able to keep in touch otherwise. My nephews live in a different state from me and FaceTiming them is the highlight of my day. I recognize the value of my phone, but I know it has limits. It can never replace person-to-person interaction.

The phone is a tool, but if we aren't careful, this tool becomes a weapon. I'm not being hyperbolic here: overuse of our phones is a relationship killer. I have chosen to let friendships fade because I'm so frustrated by their phone dependency. This device acts as a barrier to authentic human interaction, and it's a roadblock to true social relationships.

It takes courage to put away our phones. It's hard to walk into a room where we don't know many people. I know the feeling well! When we do that, we feel exposed, maybe a little ridiculous. But we have convinced ourselves that if we enter an unknown situation with our noses buried in our phones, we're protected. We think we appear busy and popular with other things, cool, unconcerned, aloof in a superior way. That's not what's happening. You're using your phone as a pacifier. Spit it out and be a grown up. Be brave. Put the phone away. Get to know the people around you. Talk to them and listen to them.

Talking and listening are essential to resetting friendships, forming new relationships, and taking current friendships to the next level. There is never a time where they're unnecessary. In order to have substantial, long-lasting friendships, we must take the time to talk and listen. Forming friendships is as simple as watering a seed and asking God for the patience to see where it grows.

Conclusion

Jesus, among infinitely other things, is a wise teacher. He knows his audience, and he caters the content of his teachings to those who are listening. While on earth, Jesus's audience was often comprised of farmers. Because of this, so many of his insights contain agricultural themes.

Here is an example. In the Gospel of John, Jesus is preparing himself to enter into Jerusalem, where he will soon be crucified. He knows what's coming. He declares: "Truly, truly, I say to you, unless a grain of wheat falls into the earth and dies, it remains alone; but if it dies, it means much fruit" (John 12:24). A few chapters later, Jesus continues this line of reasoning: "Every branch of mine that bears no fruit, He takes away, and every branch that does bear fruit He prunes, that it may bear more fruit" (John 15:2).

Here are two fundamental truths that Jesus and every agrarian person understands: death is necessary, and death leads to life.

In this book, I have encouraged you to examine your friendships. And hopefully, I have spurred you into action. Maybe you have decided to put in the effort to elevate your relationships and to make them more Christ centered. Amazing—I am so proud of you. Maybe you have committed to being more honest with your friends and expressing your genuine feelings. That's incredible—keep it up. Maybe you have realized that some of your friendships are possibly unsalvageable, and you're now taking steps away from the relationship. I admire you for being so brave.

Regardless of what you're going to do or not do, relationship transitions are challenging. Shifts in friendship deeply affect us. In some ways, the changes might feel like a death. You might feel something close to mourning. Like your friend has died. Like you have died. It's not overdramatic or silly to feel this way. Don't ridicule yourself for going through these heavy emotions.

Death can feel scary and overwhelming, but the Christian knows death is not the end. Jesus proved it. He endured agonizing suffering and a legitimate death. But after three days in the grave, Jesus left death behind and entered into new life. Jesus promises his followers the same thing. I echo the promise of the Lord.

This death you might be feeling due to friendship changes or fallouts is agonizing and real. But you can get through it. As a teenager in Missouri once told me, "You can do hard things." This is going to be hard, but it's not the end of all friendship, and it's certainly not the end of you. Yes, this process will "prune" you (John 15:2). You will experience discomfort and genuine sorrow, maybe for a long time. But because of it, you will also experience new life.

Jesus is a God who keeps his promises. Jesus is a God who knows about resurrection. Jesus is a God who gives you graces and blessings to do all he is calling you to do. And he is calling you to be brave. He is inviting you to receive what you deserve, which is right and healthy friendships. And he will be with you, every step of the way.

My dear readers, know that I am supporting you from afar. I believe in you, and I am praying for you, every single day. I know that with the grace of God and the courage that comes from him alone, your friendships will flourish.

Appendix

Maggie's Favorite Conversation Starters and Awkward-Silence Killers

Sometimes, talking about your day gets boring. Every once in a while, you need to spice up a conversation. Let me introduce you to: Maggie's Favorite Conversation Starters and Awkward-Silence Killers. These questions have helped me learn *so much* about my friends. This list can reveal a lot, even about people I have known for years. I have discussed these topics with friends while waiting in line for roller coasters, on road trips, sitting around a dinner table, at birthday parties, and on runs. No matter the setting or the group, they have always been a hit. The questions range from silly and completely ridiculous, to insightful and introspective. Take them as surface level or as deep as you like. Just make sure everyone is heard and gets a chance to share.

#1 What's your favorite form of potato? (Fries, hash browns, tater tots, etc.)

#2 If you could go back in time and hug one person from your past, who would it be?

#3 What's your first memory?

#4 Would you rather flip a coin to win a billion dollars? Or would you rather just be guaranteed a million dollars?

#5 What makes you grumpy?

#6 Would you rather only ever smell vanilla icing for the rest of your life or be unable to smell anything else ever again?

#7 What was your favorite birthday?

#8 You have to choose one: would you rather know when you're going to die or know how you're going to die?

#9 If you could have one liquid come out of your finger at any time, what liquid would that be?

#10 What's your phone background?

#11 You get $1,000 for every day that you're in prison. You don't get to choose which prison you're put in, but you can choose to leave at any time. Would you take this offer, and how many days would you last?

#12 Who was your first friend?

#13 Would you rather every song exist, but it has to be sung by Pitbull? Or would you rather every artist exist, but they can only sing Pitbull songs?

#14 How have you changed since high school? How have you stayed the same?

#15 For three months, would you rather be trapped in a Barnes and Noble or a Costco?

#16 Have you ever had a perfect day?

#17 You instantly get $50 million, but you're followed by a snail for the rest of your life. The snail knows where you are at all times, and you die an agonizing death if the snail touches you. Would you take the money and the stalker snail?

#18 What's the biggest risk you've ever taken?

#19 If you could relive one day from this past year, what would it be?

#20 If you could relive one day from the past five years, what would it be?

#21 What book do you wish you could read again for the first time?

#22 How many seagulls would you have to find in your house until you'd begin to suspect someone is hiding them there?

#23 What are your top three favorite movies?

#24 If you were stuck in an infinite time loop, what would you want to be doing?

#25 What's your favorite holiday?

#26 What's the nicest thing someone has ever said to you?

#27 If money and time weren't obstacles, where would you go and what would you do on your dream vacation?

#28 Would you rather have legs as long as your fingers or fingers as long as your legs?

#29 If you had a choice, would you rather never have to sleep or never have to breathe again?

#30 When you were little, what did you want to be when you grew up?

#31 Would you rather never use the internet ever again, or never have heating and air-conditioning ever again?

#32 What's the best gift you have ever received?

#33 If you won the lottery, what's the first purchase you would make?

#34 Would you rather be 25% happier but have to walk 25% slower?

#35 Do you believe in aliens?

#36 If aliens are real, would you want to know this for sure or not know at all?

#37 What are you most excited about in your life right now?

#38 Would you rather be a professional athlete or a professional musician?

#39 If you won $100 for every pigeon you could hold, how many pigeons could you successfully hold for at least a minute?

#40 If you had to choose right now, would you rather eat a cup of dirt or run a marathon?

#41 Walk me through your ideal day. If you had the day completely free and zero responsibilities, what would you do?

#42 Would you rather have the hiccups for the rest of your life or always feel like you're about to sneeze but physically can't?

#43 What's your perfect pizza? Build it for me: crust, sauce, cheese, toppings, etc.

#44 If you could only wear one pair of shoes that you currently own for the rest of your life, what shoes would they be?

#45 Would you rather have to say everything you think out loud or never be able to speak again?

#46 If you could instantly become an expert in something, what would it be?

#47 What's one food you hated as a child but now enjoy?

#48 Who is your role model?

Maggie Craig is a full-time Catholic speaker for adults, young adults, and teens. She speaks on topics of true friendship, authentic femininity, living the Christian life with joy and adventure, and encountering Christ in the sacraments.

Craig earned a bachelor's degree in catechetics and a master's degree in theology and Christian ministry from Franciscan University of Steubenville. Craig served as a Life Teen missionary and a middle school youth minister.

She has spoken at the Los Angeles Religious Education Congress, the National Catholic Youth Conference, the Cleveland Catholic Women's Conference, and many diocesan youth conferences.

Craig currently resides in Southern California.

Maggie-craig.com
Facebook: @maggiecraigspeaking
Instagram: @maggie_craig_catholic_speaker
YouTube: @maggiecraigcatholicspeaker
TikTok: @ maggiecraigspeaker

Emily Wilson Hussem is an international speaker, author, and YouTuber who runs a global ministry for women. She is the bestselling and award-winning author of *Go Bravely*, *Awaken My Heart*, *The Go Bravely Companion Journal*, and the *Awaken My Heart Prayer Journal*.